MUST

manual for
users of
standardized
tests

by

JONELL H. KIRBY, Ed. D.
associate professor
west virginia college of
graduate studies
institute, west virginia

WILLIAM H. CULP, Ed. D.
associate professor
west virginia college of
graduate studies
institute, west virginia

JOE KIRBY, Ed. S.
assistant professor
west virginia college of
graduate studies
institute, west virginia

STS

MEASUREMENT
EVALUATION

SCHOLASTIC TESTING SERVICE, INC.
bensenville, illinois 60106

dedicated to our parents:

CHARLIE & ALMEDIA HEMPHILL

GEORGE & GLADYS CULP

LEO & ADA KIRBY

table of contents

list of figures

PART I
STATISTICAL CONCEPTS IN
STANDARDIZED TESTING

PART II
USING TEST RESULTS

manual for users of standardized tests

INTRODUCTION

Teachers and other school personnel are sometimes confronted with test data without knowing the meaning or uses of the data. There are other times when a person — teacher, counselor, or principal, — needs to choose a test to measure a program or class without clearly specified objectives for the choice. In the first instance, the individual is at a loss in interpreting or using the data, and in the second, the individual is in a quandary because he has no basis for evaluating the "goodness" of a test.

Most schools, many school systems, and some states have a system-wide testing program whereby all school children at certain grade levels are tested. Many teachers fail to use the potentially valuable information obtained from these extensive testing programs because they have not been trained to use the data.

We have seen the need for more accessible information about testing and test interpretation; thus, this Manual for Users of Standardized Tests (MUST). We hope that we have presented enough information in a straightforward manner to prevent your feeling overwhelmed by the statistical concepts, while at the same time providing adequate information and material for effective comprehension and efficient utilization of the data. Our efforts are directed toward helping the test user understand and use test data for administrative, instructional, and guidance purposes.

ORGANIZATION OF MUST

This manual is divided into three major sections: Part I — Statistical Concepts in Standardized Testing; Part II — Using Test Results; and Part III — Ethical Standards and Issues.

The appendices include: 1. Answers to study questions for Part I; 2. Definitions of terms which include formulas and examples; 3. A test and answer key for Parts I and II; 4. Case reports — verbatim transcripts of EDS and GATB score interpretations; and 5. A selected and annotated bibliography.

Part I has study questions at the end of the discussion of each topic to help direct learning; therefore, it can be used more or less as a programmed text. Answers will be found in Appendix A. Appendix B provides a quick reference for definitions and formulas used in Part I.

Part II has "assignments" and questions for consideration which may be used for "pre-" and "post-" instructional comparisons, and a "final examination" to facilitate application of test data. Appendix C offers a test which covers material contained in Parts I and II, and Appendix D provides the answers for quick scoring. The writers of this manual also see the value of using the test contained in Appendix C for purposes of pre- and post-instructional evaluation and as a performance criterion measure for admission into certain graduate courses.

Part III is designed to stimulate thinking and discussions concerning the use of test data; therefore, it may be especially useful as a discussion guide for seminars and in-service training groups.

The case report in Appendix E is a verbatim transcript of a school counselor's interpretation of STS-EDS scores to high school students. The case report in Appendix F is a verbatim GATB interpretation by an employment counselor. After using this procedure, the counselor told the authors that both he and his clients now make far more use of test data obtained from the GATB than was true prior to his training and use of these interpretation procedures. The test user should read these case reports before beginning study of Part II.

Hopefully, MUST will be convenient for test users as a quick reference for formulas, definitions, explanations, outlines (i.e., test interpretation, test evaluation), and tables (i.e., standard error of measurement, normal distribution, comparison of test scores). In addition, the final appendix provides a selected and annotated bibliography for further readings on understanding and using standardized tests and their results.

AN OVERVIEW

In Part I the statistical bases for testing and test interpretation are discussed. Presenting this material first is running a calculated risk — the possibility of losing the student who is frightened by the word "statistics"! Unfortunately, many people permit their lives to be dominated by words. "Statistics — I can never pass that!" is a statement often heard. This attitude tends to defeat the student before he begins; with a positive attitude, the student will have no difficulty in mastering the material presented in this section.

The study of statistics involves learning a method of dealing with numbers so that they have more meaning. The test user who does not have this knowledge will not be prepared to evaluate the variety of published tests. In addition, he will be completely unable to present a meaningful interpretation of testing results to the individual who took the test.

Fortunately, the rules can easily be mastered by the average student. Although this material is usually presented in a complicated manner, we have tried to avoid this by using practical examples and minimizing the computation. It is not our intention to teach you all the computational skills of descriptive statistics; however, the working of the few short problems presented will help you understand the meaning of these techniques.

With these considerations in mind, the student should begin the study of this manual with an optimistic outlook. Think of yourself as a success, and success will come to you! We have had many years of teaching experience in this field, and have yet to find one of our students who could not master the descriptive statistics techniques and test interpretation procedures presented. The only problem we have encountered is fear — or perhaps more accurately, anxiety — and once the student has conquered this, learning has progressed rapidly. Consider yourself as a successful student of statistics and test interpretation and you will experience success in mastering the material in this manual.

J.H.K.
W.H.C.
J.E.K.

part 1
statistical concepts in standardized testing

A. ASSIGNING NUMBERS TO OBJECTS

Before we begin a discussion centering on techniques for giving meaning to numbers, it will be helpful to consider methods by which numbers are assigned to objects. *Scaling* is the term used to define this process. Scaling is the assigning of numbers to objects according to rules. Basically, there are four types of scaling: nominal, ordinal, interval, and ratio. In discussing them, let us first consider assigning numbers to indicate the height of the six individuals shown in Figure 1.

Fig. 1. Assigning Numbers According to Height

Nominal Scaling

If we classified the six individuals as either tall or short, they could be divided as illustrated in Figure 2.

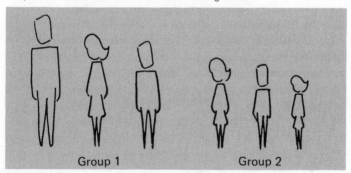

Group 1   Group 2

Fig. 2. Nominal Scaling of Height

Figure 2 would meet our requirements for scaling, as we have classified objects according to a rule — in this case, a very simple one. Now, we might assign the first group the number one and the second group the number two. This illustrates the *nominal* scaling technique. There are two basic rules for nominal scaling:
1. The objects must be classified into groups with a difference in

respect to the attributes being scaled — in this case, height; in addition, 2. an object cannot be assigned to more than one category — an individual is either in the tall group or in the short group. Notice that the numbers which we assigned to these groups have little meaning except that they define the categories to which the people have been assigned. They are like house numbers which do not imply quantity, but do give us an address or a location.

People and objects are often scaled nominally according to various types of categories; however, the measurement of height is usually not scaled in this way. Some of the common classifications might be: Democrat, Republican; male, female; urban, rural; or any other system which involves dividing people into classes based upon nominal scaling rules. The important thing to remember is that if a number is assigned to a class as the result of nominal scaling, it does not imply a quantity; it merely defines the class to which the individual belongs.

Study Questions:
1. *List several examples of nominal scaling.*
2. *Does the zip code number fulfill the requirements of nominal scaling?*

Ordinal Scaling

The rule for *ordinal* scaling is to arrange objects in order from those which have more to those which have less of some quantity. If we use height to ordinally scale the individuals used in our illustration, we could arrange them from the shortest to the tallest. We then assign them numbers, perhaps starting with the shortest and assigning that individual a "1."

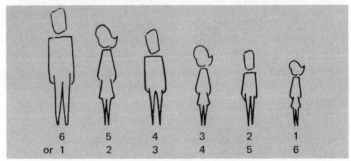

Fig. 3. Ordinal Scaling of Height

Note that we could assign the numbers in the opposite direction — giving the tallest individual a "1" and the shortest a "6." The numbers indicate the position of the individuals along a continuum as they are ordered. Figure 3 illustrates ordinal scaling.

Study Questions:
3. *List several examples of ordinal scaling.*
4. *Does arranging the Major League pitchers from highest to lowest in ERA (Earned Run Average) fulfill the requirements of ordinal scaling?*

Interval Scaling

In *interval scaling* of objects, or people, the choice of intervals is our decision and may be completely arbitrary. For example, we might decide to use the height of a garbage can as an interval on which to scale our individuals. In our example, we measure the individuals and record the number of cans necessary to reach their height. These numbers have been recorded beneath the individuals in Figure 4. Notice the advantage of this interval scaling: It gives more precision to our measurement.

| 3 | 2-2/3 | 2-1/3 | 2 | 1-3/4 | 1-1/2 |

Fig. 4. Interval Scaling of Height in "Garbage Can" Intervals

Study Questions:
5. *List several examples of interval scaling.*
6. *Is temperature on the Fahrenheit scale an example of interval scaling?*

Ratio Scaling

If we have an absolute zero, we can classify our people or objects according to a *ratio scale*. For example, our monetary system meets the requirements of ratio scaling. Not only does it meet all the requirements of interval scaling, but also it has the absolute zero. The absolute zero indicates the complete absence of the attribute; and zero money — indeed — means an absence of money. Note, on the other hand, the manner in which we

11

measure heat: Using the Fahrenheit scale, zero degrees does not imply the complete absence of heat; and on the Centigrade scale, zero degrees is the freezing point, which still does not imply the complete absence of heat. Zero point is an **agreed-upon point** on the Fahrenheit or Centigrade scales. Therefore, Fahrenheit and Centigrade scales are interval scales of temperature.

In measuring height, we have a ratio scaling technique that we can use. Our usual system of measuring height according to inches and feet, where zero **does** imply the absence of height, is a ratio-scaling technique. Figure 5 gives the ratio scaling of our six individuals according to height. Notice the different meaning that these numbers have: They now are more precise.

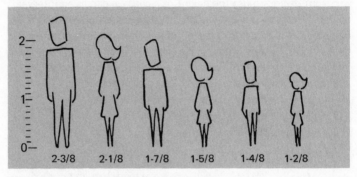

Fig. 5. Ratio Scaling of Height

Study Questions:
7. List several examples of ratio scaling.
8. Could temperature be scaled on a ratio scale?

Summary

In this section the four types of scaling were presented: *nominal scaling*, where the individuals are divided into categories according to some rule, and where the numbers assigned to these categories define the categories and have no other meaning; *ordinal scaling*, where the individuals are arranged in order according to the attributes on which they are being scaled, and where numbers are assigned to the individuals in accordance to their position in the order; *interval scaling*, where individuals are measured according to a specified unit, and numbers are assigned to the individuals according to how much they measure in terms of that unit; and, finally, *ratio scaling*, where all of the requirements of the previous scaling techniques are met and, in addition, we have an absolute zero point established.

What type of scaling do we have in test data or test results? It would certainly appear that in most cases we have met the requirements of ordinal scaling. Have we met the requirements of inverval scaling? No, not in most cases. However, we approach the interval scaling requirements, and it is often appropriate to assume that we have achieved this level of scaling.

B. ORGANIZING NUMBERS FOR MEANING

Suppose we gave a classroom test to ten students. The test consisted of eight arithmetic problems, and we scored the tests according to the number of problems the students worked correctly. The scores of our class of ten students are: 5, 7, 1, 5, 3, 2, 4, 4, 6, and 4. What do these scores mean? How can we organize these numbers so that the scores will have more meaning? How can we communicate the meaning of these numbers to others? These are the questions that will be discussed in this section.

Frequency Tables

Our first step in organizing this series of numbers involves arranging the scores from the lowest to the highest. In this particular case, we would start with the lowest score, which is 1, and rearrange our scores from low to high (that is, ordinal scaling). The next step is to count the number of times each score was obtained, i.e., the frequency of each score. In the first column of Figure 6, we started with the low score of 1 and worked up to the high score of 7. In the second column, we recorded the number of times that particular score was obtained by the students who took the test.

Test Scores	Frequency f
7	1
6	1
5	2
4	3
3	1
2	1
1	1
	$N = 10$

Fig. 6. Arrangement of Test Scores: Frequency Table

From this *frequency table* we can see that the score of 1 was obtained by only one student, while the score of 4 was obtained by three students, and the score of 5 was obtained by two students. The second column, labeled with a small letter *"f,"* indicates the frequency — the number of times — that score was obtained. We now know more about these numbers than previously. For example, we know the score of 4 was obtained by more students than any other single score. And, we know the highest score was 7 and the lowest score was 1.

Study Questions:
9. How many students obtained a raw score of 3?
10. The scores obtained by nine students on a classroom examination are: 5, 2, 3, 1, 4, 2, 3, 3, 4. Complete a frequency table for these data. (You will do well to keep your work on this question; later study questions will use these same scores in practicing other statistical techniques.)

Graphing

We would have a much better idea of what these numbers mean if we were to draw a picture of them. This is usually called *graphing* the data. Graphing represents the data in the form of a picture so that we can understand more of the meaning the numbers have and then convey this meaning to others. Although there are many types of graphs, only one is presented here. (The student who desires more information on graphic techniques should consult a standard statistics book.) It is usually the practice to begin by representing all possible scores as points along a line. Figure 7 shows a horizontal line for scores that ranged from 1 to 7. Notice that we have included all of the obtained scores on this line and one additional score at each end.

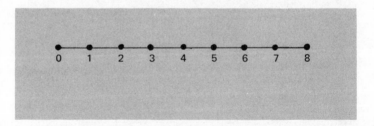

Fig. 7. Graphing Data: Scores on Horizontal Line

If we wanted to represent individual scores along the line, we would place an "X" above the score for every individual who obtained that score. This has been done in Figure 8.

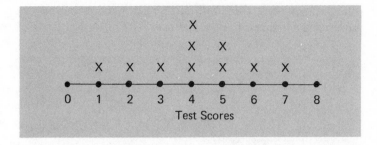

Fig. 8. Graphing Data: Individual Scores Represented by X's

The number of X's correspond to the number of people who obtained each of these scores, and the total number of X's is the same as the total number of people taking the test ($N = 10$).

With a large group of data it is cumbersome to represent each individual score with an "X," so an alternative method is used. We simply draw a vertical line, called the vertical axis, with an agreed-upon standard interval marking to represent the number or frequency of individual scores along the axis. Notice how this has been done in Figure 9.

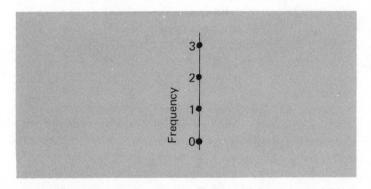

Fig. 9. Graphing Data: Vertical Axis to Represent Frequency of Scores

The usual rule for determining the length of the vertical line or axis is that it should be two thirds to three fourths the length of the horizontal line or axis.

If we place the vertical axis and horizontal axis together, as has been done in Figure 10, we can graph our data without using an "X" to represent each score. Remember, the height of the vertical axis for any score is determined by the number of students who obtain this particular score. When we join the

points representing the numbers obtaining each score, we have
constructed a frequency polygon, as shown in Figure 10.

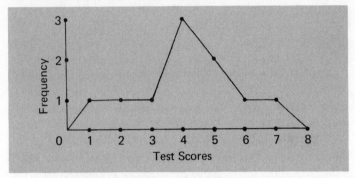

Fig. 10. Graphing Data: Frequency Polygon

Study Questions:
11. a. *In graphing, what do we usually represent on the
       horizontal axis?*
    b. *What do we usually represent on the vertical axis?*
    c. *What is our usual rule for determining the height of
       the vertical axis?*
    d. *What is a frequency polygon?*
12. *Draw a frequency polygon for the scores listed in
    Study Question 10.*

Interval Sizes

When we have a large number of scores with a wide range,
it is usually desirable to divide them into intervals before we construct our frequency polygon. For example, if the lowest score
were 5 and the highest 49, it would be difficult to construct a
frequency polygon to include this range of scores. (The *range*
is the highest minus the lowest plus one, or 45 in this case.) It is
the usual procedure to have approximately 15 intervals, so an
interval size (i) of 3 would be appropriate in this problem ($i = 3$).
To keep our illustrations simple, we will not deal with wide ranges
or large samples; however, the student should be aware of this
method of grouping data by using intervals.

Apparent and Real Limits

Before continuing with our discussion, it is necessary to
point out two properties of the numbers which were graphed in
the previous section (see Figure 10). The *apparent limits* of a
number are those indicated by the number. For example, in

16

Figure 10 it appears that a student can obtain a score of 5, or 6, or 3, or some other whole number, and that these are the limits of the score. However, scores obtained on a test are in reality continuous. That is, a score actually lies between two numbers. The real limits of a number extend one-half a unit below and one-half a unit above the number. For example, the number three has the real limits of 2.5 and 3.5 — or, to say it another way, 3 is the midpoint which implies 2.5 to 3.5. The *apparent limits* and *real limits* for an interval size of 3 ($i = 3$) are illustrated in Figure 11. The apparent limits of the interval 7 - 9 are the scores 7, 8, and 9, but the real limits of the interval are 6.5 and 9.5.

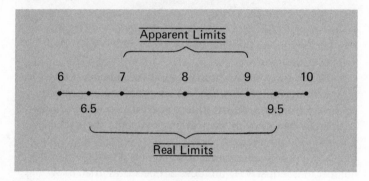

Fig. 11. Apparent and Real Limits

Study Questions:
13. a. *What is the range of scores when the lowest score is 2 and the highest is 46?*
    b. *What interval size would you use for these scores?*
    c. *What are the apparent and real limits of the number 4?*
    d. *What are the apparent and real limits of the interval 2–4?*
    e. *In the interval 2–4,* i = ?

Cumulative Frequency Distributions

Now, let us return to our original data and talk about the *cumulative frequency*. To obtain the cumulative frequency, we add the numbers for each successive category. This number, therefore, tells us the *total number* of people who scored below the *upper real limits* of that particular interval.

In Figure 12, the raw score, the frequency, and the cumulative frequency are given for our original set of data. Notice that each of the cumulative frequencies represents the addition of all those frequencies below the upper real limits of the particular interval.

Test Score	f	cf	Computation
7	1	10	(9 + 1 = 10)
6	1	9	(8 + 1 = 9)
5	2	8	(6 + 2 = 8)
4	3	6	(3 + 3 = 6)
3	1	3	(2 + 1 = 3)
2	1	2	(1 + 1 = 2)
1	1	1	(1 + 0 = 1)
	N = 10		

Fig. 12. Computing Cumulative Frequency (*cf*)

There are two ways of calculating the cumulative frequency for a given interval. We can add all of the frequencies beneath the upper real limit of that interval, or we can add the cumulative frequency of the previous interval to the frequency of this interval. Our last entry in the cumulative frequency column — the top number — must be the total number of people, i.e., the number must equal *N*. If this does not occur, we then know we have made an error.

Study Questions:
14. Compute the cumulative frequency column for the scores listed in Study Question 10.

Percentiles

The most commonly used technique for representing the relative position of an individual's score in a group of scores is the percentile rank. If a student has a raw score of 52 on a test, what does this mean? The raw score does not tell us what the highest score was on the examination, nor does it tell us the lowest. If we knew the position this score had in relation to the other scores on the test, it would have more meaning for us.

We have already computed the cumulative frequency column for our scores, and we could report this. However, it is more meaningful to talk about the position of an individual's score when it is compared to a standard number of individuals. This is usually done by the percentile, which makes the assumption that there are one hundred scores which are being compared. It is not necessary to have exactly one hundred scores — we can have more or less, and this causes us no problem. To convert the cumulative frequency column into percentiles, the first step is to divide the cumulative frequency by the total number of people included in the distribution. In this case our total N was ten; therefore, we divide each entry in the cumulative frequency column by ten.

(1) Test Score	(2) f	(3) cf	(4) $100\left(\dfrac{cf}{N}\right)$	(5) Percentile Rank
7	1	10	10/10 x 100	100
6	1	9	9/10 x 100	90
5	2	8	8/10 x 100	80
4	3	6	6/10 x 100	60
3	1	3	3/10 x 100	30
2	1	2	2/10 x 100	20
1	1	1	1/10 x 100	10
	$N = 10$			

Fig. 13. Computation of Percentiles

Notice that the highest score in Figure 13 is ten divided by ten, which is one. (If this is not the case, we have made an error in our computations.) To eliminate the problem of using decimals, and to compare individuals to an N of one hundred, multiply by one hundred. The result is a percentage which tells us the percentage of the people who scored below the upper real limit of the interval in which the raw score was located (See Figure 13). For example, we know that a student whose raw score is 4 would have a percentile score of 60, or that 60 percent of the individuals fell below the upper real limits of this interval.

Study Questions:
15. *Compute the percentile column for the scores for Study Question 10.*
16. *What does the percentile rank tell us?*

The Ogive

It is sometimes desirable to graph the percentile rank as we did the raw scores in Figure 10. If this is done, we represent the raw scores along the horizontal axis as was done previously and the percentiles along the vertical axis. In Figure 14, the percentiles calculated in Figure 13 have been graphed; the resulting curve is called an ***ogive***.

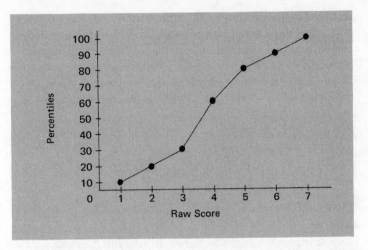

Fig. 14. Graph Showing Raw Scores and Percentile Ranks — Ogive

The value of this graph, the ogive, is that we can now easily read percentile equivalents. If a student obtained a raw score of 4, for example, we would follow the vertical line from the score of 4 up until it intersects the ogive. We then follow the horizontal line to the percentile rank, 60. The reverse procedure would be used to read a raw score if the percentile were given. For example, the percentile equivalent for a raw score of 5.5 is about 85, and the raw score equivalent for a percentile rank of 50 is about 3.7.

Summary

In this section, several methods of organizing data to give our scores meaning and to convey this meaning to others were presented. Although the number of individuals in the sample used was small, several methods of organizing these data were illustrated to show the procedures used in graphing and calculating percentiles.

The scores were organized from high to low, and the *frequency* was tabulated for each score. The scores were then *graphed* to obtain a picture of the scores. The *cumulative frequency* was then calculated by adding the frequency of each preceding score. The *percentile* was then computed to provide a standardized measure — the number of people out of one hundred who scored below the interval in which a particular individual scored. Finally, the percentile ranks and raw scores were graphed as an *ogive*, which permits direct look-ups of intervening (unplotted) raw scores or percentile ranks.

C. MEASURES OF CENTRAL TENDENCY

Returning to the picture which we drew for our data in Figure 10, we can see that it would be convenient if we could have a point to indicate the center of this graph. Then, by referring to this point, we could tell whether an individual score was above or below it. Finding the central point will be discussed in this section. Basically, there are three commonly used central points or measures of central tendency: the mode, the median, and the mean.

The Mode

The *mode* is simply the score which is obtained most frequently. In our illustration, there were three people who obtained a raw score of 4. Since more people obtained this raw score, more than any other single raw score, we say that this is the mode.

Study Questions:
17. *What is the mode for the data given in Study Question 10?*
18. *The mode is the _____ frequently obtained score.*

The Median

The *median* is the fiftieth percentile, or the point which divides our group into two equal parts: Half of the people score above this point, and half score below this point. In many distributions, there will be a score exactly equivalent to the fiftieth percentile; however, in many other cases, there will not be.

Test Score	f	Cumulative cf	Percentile Rank	
7	1	10	100	
6	1	9	90	
5	2	8	80	
4	3	6	60	
?	. . . .			50
3	1	3	30	
2	1	2	20	
1	1	1	10	

Fig. 15. Fiftieth Percentile Not Represented by Raw Score

Notice that the raw score for the fiftieth percentile is not given in Figure 15. A raw score of 3 had a percentile rank of 30 and a raw score of 4 had a percentile rank of 60. We know that the fiftieth percentile would be greater than the upper real limit of the raw score of 3 (which is 3.5), and it would be less than the upper real limit of 4 (which is 4.5). The fiftieth percentile may be determined by interpolation. To compute the fiftieth percentile, a simple variation of an algebraic system of interpolation may be used.

Interpolation

To find the raw score for the fiftieth percentile by interpolation from Figure 15, we write the percentiles between which it must lie, and their raw score equivalents in terms of their upper real limits. Thus the fiftieth percentile lies between percentiles 60 and 30, which correspond to raw scores 4 and 3, whose upper real limits are 4.5 and 3.5.

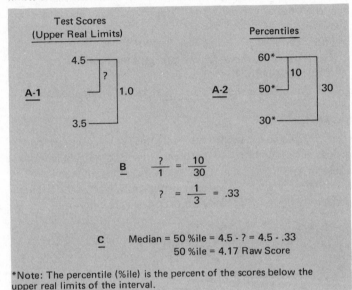

*Note: The percentile (%ile) is the percent of the scores below the upper real limits of the interval.

Fig. 16. Method of Interpolation

We know the distance between percentiles 60 and 50 is 10 and the distance between percentiles 60 and 30 is 30. These distances are written beside these numbers in A-2 of Figure 16. We also know that the distance between 4.5 and 3.5 is 1, but we *do not know* how far from 4.5 our particular score will be, so we represent this distance with a question mark as shown in A-1 of Figure 16.

Notice that we have drawn a large "box" and a small "box" to represent the distances in the problem, and since we do not

22

know the size of the small box in A-1 of Figure 16, we indicate this with a question mark.

These distances may be written as fractions by putting the small box distances in the numerator, and the large box distances in the denominator. If we place an equal sign between these two fractions, we have a simple algebraic problem as shown in Figure 16 B. Now the problem is easily worked, because we know that any number divided by one would be that same number, so that ? divided by 1 is equal to ?. And on the other side of the equation we have one third, which is equal to the decimal .33. The .33 is the distance from the upper real limit of the interval 4.5 where this median is located, so we subtract .33 from 4.5, giving us 4.17. Therefore, this *median* or *fiftieth percentile* is equal to a raw score of 4.17.

However, we sometimes do not have such a simple problem to work, so the complete steps in working the problem are illustrated. In algebra a question mark is usually not used. The use of the small letter *"x"* to represent an unknown number is standard, so that will be used in the next sample. (Note: *x* = ? in this example)

If you will think of the equal sign as the center of a scale where you must do the same thing to both sides of the scale in order to keep it in balance, there will be little difficulty in working this problem. Basically, we want to manipulate our equation so that we have the letter *"x"* on one side, and the numbers on the other side. To do this we must do something to the denominator of the *left-hand side* of our equation. If we multiply both sides by one, we could eliminate the fraction *x*/1 by dividing it out (this number will usually not be one but, as we pointed out earlier, this illustration is trying to generalize to a situation where you would have a more difficult problem).

$$1 \times \frac{x}{1} = \frac{10}{30} \times 1$$

$$x = \frac{10}{30}$$

Fig. 17. Algebraic Interpolation

On the other side, we now have *"x"* equal to ten over thirty, which gives us our *"x"* on one side of the equation and our numbers on the other side. We now divide our fraction 10/30, obtaining the .33. This is the same result that we obtained in the previous problem.

Now, let's look at a slightly different problem. We have grouped data with an interval size of 3, and we would like to report the median. However, the fiftieth percentile cannot be located, as it does not correspond with the upper limits of our intervals. Part of the problem is repeated in Figure 18.

Raw Score	%ile
15 - 17	70
12 - 14	40

Fig. 18. Locating the Median

We know that the median is greater than the upper real limit of the 12-14 interval (14.5), as this interval has a percentile rank of 40. We therefore conclude that the fiftieth percentile must be located somewhere in the 15-17 interval, between the lower real limit of 14.5 and the upper real limit of 17.5. To locate the exact point where it falls we must interpolate using these values (14.5 and 17.5). Note that the percentile value of 14.5 is 40.

Study Questions:
19. *Complete the interpolation for the problem presented in Figure 18. What is the median?*
20. *Calculate the median for the data in Study Question 10.*
21. *Define "median" in such a way that a person untrained in statistics could understand the concept.*

The Mean

The teacher who is presented with a set of test scores and asked to find the average of these scores would have no difficulty in adding them and dividing by the number of scores added. On the other hand, if he were asked to find the *mean* of a set of test scores, he might experience a feeling of incompetency and anticipate difficulty. However, the two systems are identical. The *mean* is a name given to the arithmetic average. The mean is represented by the formula in Figure 19.

$$M = \frac{\Sigma X}{N}$$

Fig. 19. Formula for the Mean

In this formula, "X" is used to represent each individual's score; "M" is used to represent the mean; "Σ" is used to indicate that all of the scores are added; and "N" is used to refer to the number of scores. The only new symbol used in this expression is the "Σ." It is much more convenient to write "Σ" than to write in words "the sum of," so this symbol is used to represent that English statement. Now there will be no problem computing the mean for our illustrative problem. We add the scores $7 + 6 + 5 + 5 + 4 + 4 + 4 + 3 + 2 + 1$ to obtain a total of 41. This is our sum of "X" or ΣX. We divide this 41 by our total number of scores ($N = 10$) to obtain our mean, which 4.1.

Study Questions:
22. *What does the sign Σ tell you to do?*
23. *You are given the scores 2, 6, 3, 1. What is ΣX?*
24. *Compute the mean for the data in Study Question 10.*
25. *What is the mean of the scores 2, 6, 3, and 1?*
26. *What is the median of the scores 2, 6, 3, and 1?*
27. *Compare the mean and median for the scores given in Study Questions 25 and 26. Is the mean a fair measure of central tendency?*
28. *Suppose you were a teacher in a small school and your salary is $7000 a year. The two other teachers in your school are also making $7000 a year, but the principal is making $11,000 a year. You ask the school for an increase in salary. They deny your request on the grounds that the average salary for your school is $8000, which is above the national average. What statistic could you report to them to more accurately describe the salary structure?*

Grade Equivalents

On achievement tests, grade equivalents are sometimes reported: John obtained a grade equivalent of 5.5 on the Arithmetic Achievement Test. What does this statement say? If John is in the sixth grade, does this indicate that he is "retarded" in arithmetic? Let us examine the usual procedure for computing grade equivalency scores so that we can answer this question intelligently.

The procedure is to assume a value of 5.0 for the typical student in the first month of the fifth grade, a 5.5 for a student in the middle of the fifth grade, and so forth. Now, to compute grade norms on an arithmetic test, the test is first administered to a sample of students at a certain grade level. Let us assume that we are administering our test to the fifth grade in the middle of the year (5.5) and to the sixth grade at the same time (6.5). After administering the test, we calculate the mean for each group. The fifth-graders scored a mean of 27 and the sixth-graders scored a mean of 47. But when we construct our norm tables, we want to have norm scores for all raw scores, and we would like to infer grade norms for students who are not in the middle of the school year. A common procedure for doing this is to interpolate the scores between the two means. Notice the example given in Figure 20.

Interval	Grade Equivalent	Interpolated Score	Obtained Mean Raw Score
	6.5		– 47
10	6.4	– 45	
9	6.3	– 43	
8	6.2	– 41	
7	6.1	– 39	
6	6.0	– 37	
5	5.9	– 35	
4	5.8	– 33	
3	5.7	– 31	
2	5.6	– 29	
1	5.5		– 27

Fig. 20. Grade Equivalents

The difference between the sixth-grade mean and the fifth-grade mean is 20 (47 – 27). We have ten intervals to which we must assign raw scores: the interval from 5.5 to 5.6, 5.6 to 5.7, etc. Figure 20 shows that there are ten of these intervals. Twenty divided by ten equals two, so we would increment each score by two raw score units. This has been done in our example, although in practice it is a more complicated procedure. However, it is not important to learn to calculate grade equivalent scores from raw scores.

There are several important considerations which should be noted in using grade equivalents. First, the only scores which are measured in our example are the grade equivalent scores of 6.5 and 5.5; the other scores are inferred. And, 47 is the mean of the sixth-grade class at the middle of the sixth-grade year, and this score has all of the characteristics of the mean. Thus, if the sample is large enough and normally distributed, we would expect that *half of the students would score below this raw score*. The teacher who says "I have a very slow group this year because only one half of them scored a grade equivalent equal to or higher than the grade to which they are assigned" does not understand the grade equivalent score. Fortunately, the grade equivalent as a method of reporting the results of a standardized test is not widely used today. It can be a very misleading concept, and we have much better ways of reporting the results to teachers and parents. There are more precise methods available for reporting test scores: one is percentiles, which have already been discussed, and another, the standard score, will be discussed in a later section.

Summary

In this section we computed three measures of *central tendency*: the *mode*, which is the score most frequently obtained; the *median*, which is the middle score or the fiftieth percentile; and the *mean*, which is the arithmetic average. In actual practice, the mode is rarely computed because it has little meaning with large groups of data. The median is the accepted measure of central tendency where we have *ordinal* data, since it is not influenced by extreme scores, which is its main advantage. The mean can be used as a measure of central tendency where we have *interval* or *ratio* data. It lends itself to further statistical analysis and is our *most stable measure* of central tendency. Although it is not always appropriate, the mean is the measure of central tendency which is usually calculated and given in standardized test manuals. The grade equivalent score was also discussed and some of its limitations were presented.

D. MEASURES OF VARIABILITY

In Figure 21, three sets of data have been graphed. All three of these graphs have the same center, but they have differences in the spread of the graph. We might say that one of them is skinny, one is normal, and one is fat. (Note: It would be more accurate statistically to say that one is leptokurtic, one is mesokurtic, and one is platykurtic.)

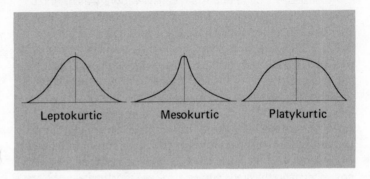

Leptokurtic   Mesokurtic   Platykurtic

Fig. 21. Frequency Polygons for Three Sets of Data

The problem in this chapter is to find a measure to express the variability of a graph so that we can communicate this difference in the spread of the graph of our data to others.

The Semi-Interquartile Range

When we have ordinal data, the measure of variability which is usually considered is the *semi-interquartile range*. The semi-interquartile range is defined as the third quartile (Q_3 or the 75th percentile) minus the first quartile (Q_1 or the 25th percentile) with the result of this subtraction divided by two. In other words, the semi-interquartile range is one half the distance between the first and third quartiles. This is summarized in the formula below.

$$Q = \frac{Q_3 - Q_1}{2}$$

Fig. 22. Formula for the Semi-Interquartile Range

The test data which were presented in Figure 13 are repeated in Figure 23, for use in an example of deriving the semi-interquartile range.

Test Score	Percentile
7	100
6	90
5	80
4	60
3	30
2	20
1	10

Fig. 23. Raw Scores and Equivalent Percentile Ranks

To calculate the semi-interquartile range, Q, for this problem, it would first be necessary to calculate the 25th and 75th percentiles. The first step, then, is to answer the questions What is Q_1 or the 25th percentile? and What is Q_3 or the 75th percentile?

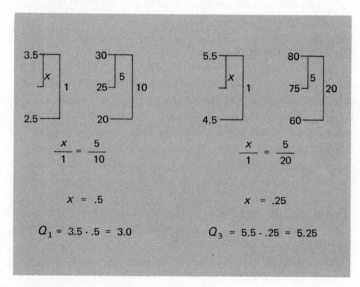

$$\frac{x}{1} = \frac{5}{10}$$

$$\frac{x}{1} = \frac{5}{20}$$

$$x = .5$$

$$x = .25$$

$$Q_1 = 3.5 - .5 = 3.0$$

$$Q_3 = 5.5 - .25 = 5.25$$

Fig. 24. Computation of Q_1 and Q_3

Q_1 or the 25th percentile is 3, and Q_3 or the 75th percentile is 5.25. The semi-interquartile range is then easily computed, as in Figure 25.

$$Q = \frac{Q_3 - Q_1}{2}$$

$$= \frac{5.25 - 3.00}{2}$$

$$= 1.13$$

Fig. 25. Computing the Semi-Interquartile Range

Since the semi-interquartile range uses percentiles, it is not difficult to remember and understand why this is appropriate for ordinal data.

Study Questions:
29. a. *Compute Q_3 for the data in Study Question 10.*
    b. *Compute Q_1 for the same data.*
    c. *What is the semi-interquartile range for these data?*
    d. *When do we use the semi-interquartile range as a measure of variability?*

The Standard Deviation
With interval or ratio data, or when we can assume that the data are distributed intervally, we can calculate the **standard deviation**. This is the most widely used measure of variability. As the name implies, the standard deviation is the deviation of each score around a standard, i.e., the mean. The formula for the standard deviation is given in Figure 26.

$$S = \sqrt{\frac{\Sigma x^2}{N}}$$

Fig. 26. Formula for the Standard Deviation

In this formula, S is the symbol for the standard deviation; x^2 is the squared deviation of the score from the mean ($x = X - M$); Σx^2 indicates the addition of all squared deviations; N is the total number of scores; and $\sqrt{}$ is the operation of obtaining the square root.

Notice that Σx^2 is *not* the same as ΣX^2. The Σx^2 indicates that we must subtract the mean, M, from each of our raw scores, X, and then square each of these differences (deviations). Then the squared differences are added. An illustration will help the student understand this operation. Let us use the set of raw scores listed in Figure 27.

X	x $(X-M)$	x^2
7	3	9
6	2	4
5	1	1
4	0	0
3	-1	1
2	-2	4
1	-3	9
$\Sigma X = 28$		$\Sigma x^2 = 28$

$$M = \frac{\Sigma X}{N}$$

$$M = \frac{28}{7}$$

$$M = 4$$

$$S = \sqrt{\frac{\Sigma x^2}{N}}$$

$$S = \sqrt{\frac{28}{7}}$$

$$S = \sqrt{4}$$

$$S = 2$$

Fig. 27. Computing the Mean (M) and Standard Deviation (S)

Notice that the first column is labeled X to represent the raw score, as we have done previously. The first step is to calculate the mean of this set of scores. (The student should complete this to review the process covered in the last chapter.) The sum of scores is 28, the N is 7, and the mean is 4.

Now that we have obtained the mean, we can construct the second column, which represents the result of subtracting the mean from the given scores. This column is labeled x or $(X - M)$.

To complete the third column, we square each entry in the second column. Remember, in algebra a − 3 times a − 3 will give us a + 9, so the final entry in this column is a + 9. Next, add the column to obtain the sum of the small x's squared ($\Sigma x^2 = 28$).

Returning to the formula presented previously, we can replace Σx^2 by 28, and N by 7. We now have S equal to the square root of 28 divided by 7. Completing this process, we have S equal to the square root of 4; the square root of 4 is 2; so S is equal to 2. In other words, our standard deviation for this set of data is 2.

Study Questions:
30. *What is the difference between x and X?*
31. *a. When is it appropriate to compute the standard deviation?*
    b. Give the formula and list the steps you must follow in computing the standard deviation.
32. *Compute the standard deviation for the data in Study Question 10.*

We do not always have a whole number for the mean. When this situation arises, we have a formula for computing the standard deviation which is easier to use when the mean contains a decimal. This formula is given in Figure 28.

$$S = \sqrt{\frac{\Sigma X^2}{N} - M^2}$$

Fig. 28. Raw Score Formula for the Standard Deviation

We approach the problem in a slightly different manner when we use this formula. We must calculate the mean and the ΣX^2. For the ΣX^2 value we must return to our *raw scores*, square each of them, then add them.

X $(N = 7)$	X^2
7	49
6	36
5	25
4	16
3	9
2	4
1	1
$M = 4$	$\Sigma X^2 = 140$

Fig. 29. Computing X^2

In Figure 29, the raw scores are given in the first column. In the second column, the squares of these scores are given; and adding the second column we get ΣX^2, which is 140.

Now, using this sum in our formula as illustrated in Figure 30, we obtain the standard deviation of 2, which is identical to the one obtained by the method presented earlier.

$$S = \sqrt{\frac{\Sigma X^2}{N} - M^2}$$

$$S = \sqrt{\frac{140}{7} - (4)^2}$$

$$S = \sqrt{20 - 16}$$

$$S = \sqrt{4}$$

$$S = 2$$

Fig. 30. Computing S Using X^2 and M

This second process appears to be complicated; however, it is easily performed with an ordinary desk or pocket calculator.

Study Questions:
33. *When would you use the raw score method to compute the standard deviation?*
34. *What is X^2?*
35. *Using the raw score method, calculate the standard deviation for the data given in Study Question 10.*

Summary

In this section two measures of variability were discussed: 1. the semi-interquartile range, which is half the distance between the first and third quartiles, and 2. the standard deviation, which is the square root of the deviation of raw scores around the mean. Variability is usually measured by the standard deviation, and this is the measure which is normally reported in test manuals.

E. THE NORMAL CURVE

In an earlier chapter the graphing of data was discussed, and the drawing of a frequency polygon for a set of data from a small sample was presented. This frequency polygon begins to smooth out and take the appearance of what is usually referred to as the *normal curve* as our sample size increases. The curve has an equation and mathematical properties which are beyond the scope of this manual, but it is important that the student have certain information available about this important curve.

The usual procedure in standardized testing is to assign a value of *zero to the central point* on this curve, which is the mean, and to assign a value of *one for each standard deviation* from the mean. In Figure 31, a zero has been placed on the line that represents the middle of the curve; the standard deviations going to the right have been assigned plus numbers; and the standard deviations going to the left have been assigned minus numbers.

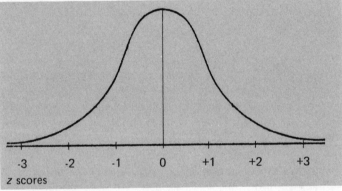

| -3 | -2 | -1 | 0 | +1 | +2 | +3 |

z scores

Fig. 31. The Normal Curve

Before continuing the discussion of the normal curve, a formula which will enable the student to calculate normal curve scores, i.e., *z* scores, from raw scores will be presented. This formula is very simple and uses the material which has been presented previously. The formula for *z* scores is given in Figure 32.

$$z = \frac{X - M}{S} = \frac{x}{S}$$

Fig. 32. Formula for Computing *z* Scores

In this formula **X** – **M** refers to the deviation score *x*, which is calculated by subtracting the mean from the raw score, and **S** refers to the standard deviation. For example, if we had a raw score of 7 and a mean of 4, with a standard deviation of 2, as we did in the example in the last chapter, we would have the following computations for **z** (See Figure 33).

$$z = \frac{X - M}{S}$$

$$z = \frac{7 - 4}{2}$$

$$z = \frac{3}{2} = 1.50$$

Fig. 33. Computing *z* Scores

With this information, we can now compare the results of two tests which have **different means** and **different standard deviations**. We can determine which raw score is higher by converting the raw scores into *z* scores. For example, say Johnny has a raw score of 10 on a spelling test which had a mean of 6 and a standard deviation of 4; and he had a raw score of 8 on an arithmetic test which had a mean of 2 and a standard deviation of 3. It would be impossible to compare these two test scores unless we converted both of them into *z*-score form. This is done for you in Figure 34.

Spelling	Arithmetic
$z = \dfrac{10 - 6}{4}$	$z = \dfrac{8 - 2}{3}$
$z = 1.00$	$z = 2.00$

Fig. 34. Comparing Scores from Two Different Tests

Notice that although Johnny's raw score was much higher on the first test, his *z* score was lower — in reality he did much better on the second test than he did on the first test. You now understand why **z** scores are necessary to give meaning to the raw test scores.

Study Questions:
36. *A z score has a mean of _____ and a standard deviation of _____.*
37. *A z score to the right of the mean has a _____ sign, and one to the left has a _____ sign.*
38. *If you had M = 4, and S = 2, what would be the z scores for the following raw scores: 6, 5, 4, 3, 2, 1?*

Additional Information About the Normal Curve

With a little additional information about the normal curve, we can also give greater meaning to the **z** score. If 100 people took a test, and the distribution followed the shape of a normal curve, we would find that *approximately* 34 people would score between the mean and one standard deviation, approximately 14 people would score between the first standard deviation and the second standard deviation, and approximately 2 people would score between the second standard deviation and the third standard deviation. The curve in Figure 35 illustrates this property of the normal curve. (Note: The percentages are actually 34.1, 13.6, and 2.1, but for our purposes the figures given will be close enough.)

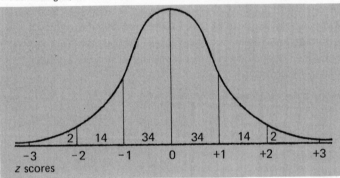

Fig. 35. The Normal Curve

If you recall what you have learned about percentiles, you will see that the percentile is not directly comparable to the **z** score. Recalling our discussion of the treatment of ordinal data and the treatment of interval data, you will realize why this is true — percentiles are ordinal data and **z** scores are interval data. Figure 36 shows the relationship.

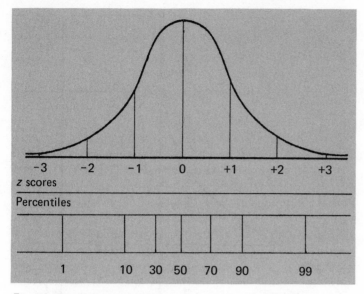

Fig. 36. The Relationship Between *z* Scores and Percentiles

It is sometimes difficult for test users to deal with the negative *z* score and the decimals that are involved when the *z* score is not a whole number. For this reason most standardized tests convert the *z* score into a number which does not have these characteristics. For example, the Stanford-Binet Intelligence Scale has a mean of 100 and a standard deviation of 16, and the Wechsler Adult Intelligence Scale has a mean of 100 and a standard deviation of 15. The conversion of *z* scores to a different unit, i.e., *T* scores, is easily accomplished using the formula in Figure 37.

For your convenience, Figure 38 presents the relationships between various standard score systems.

In studying Figure 38, it is important to note that scores on different tests are ***not*** directly comparable. For example, a deviation IQ score of 70 cannot be interpreted as being equivalent to a ***CEEB*** score of 300.

$$T = M + zS$$

Fig. 37. Formula for Converting *z* Scores to *T* Scores

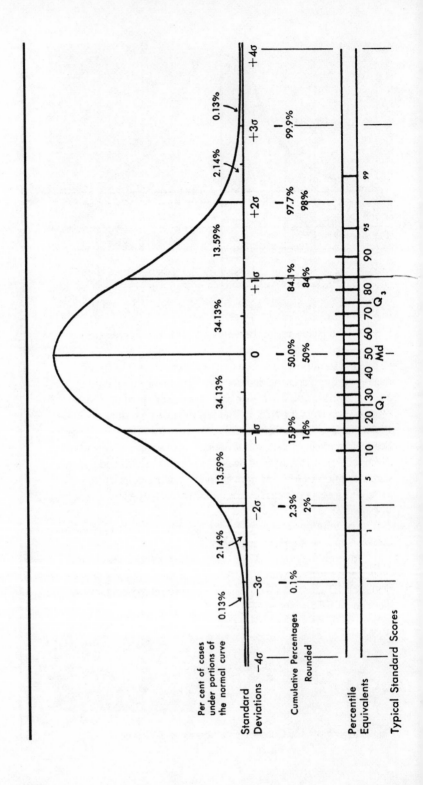

Per cent of cases under portions of the normal curve

Standard Deviations −4σ −3σ −2σ −1σ 0 +1σ +2σ +3σ +4σ

0.13%   2.14%   13.59%   34.13%   34.13%   13.59%   2.14%   0.13%

Cumulative Percentages   0.1%   2.3%   15.9%   50.0%   84.1%   97.7%   99.9%
Rounded   2%   16%   50%   84%   98%

Percentile Equivalents
1   5   10   20 30 40 50 60 70 80   90   95   99
Q₁   Md   Q₃

Typical Standard Scores

NOT USED ON PROFILES

z-scores	-4.0	-3.0	-2.0		-1.0	0	+1.0	+2.0	+3.0	+4.0

MMPI T-scores: 20, 30, 40, 50, 60, 70, 80

GRE, SAT CEEB scores: 200, 300, 400, 500, 600, 700, 800

AGCT scores: 40, 60, 80, 100, 120, 140, 160

Stanines: 1, 2, 3, 4, 5, 6, 7, 8, 9

Per cent in stanine: 4%, 7%, 12%, 17%, 20%, 17%, 12%, 7%, 4%

Wechsler Scales
Subtests: 1, 4, 7, 10, 13, 16, 19

WISC / WAIS

Deviation IQs: 55, 70, 85, 100, 115, 130, 145

NOTE: This chart cannot be used to equate scores on one test to scores on another test. For example, both 600 on the CEEB and 120 on the AGCT are one standard deviation above their respective means, but they do not represent "equal" standings because the scores were obtained from different groups.

(From: *Test Service Bulletin No. 48*, Psychological Corporation, January, 1955.)

Fig. 38. A Comparison of Several Ways of Reporting Test Scores

STEN (STANDARD TEN)

In this formula, T represents the new score, M represents the new mean which has been arbitrarily set, z represents the z score as previously discussed, and S represents the standard deviation. Now if we had a z score of 1 and wanted to convert this to the Wechsler Adult Intelligence Scale system, we could replace these values in our formula as shown in Figure 39.

$$IQ \; T = M + zS$$

$$IQ \; T = 100 + (1)15$$

$$IQ \; T = 115$$

Fig. 39. Converting z Scores to T Scores

The new mean which we are seeking is 100, the z score which we have calculated from our raw score data is 1, and the S that we are seeking is 15. Therefore, the T score or new score would be 115.

Study Questions:
39. *In a normal distribution, what percentages of cases will fall between*
    a. *a z score of -1 and a z score of +1?*
    b. *a z score of +1 and a z score of +3?*
    c. *a z score of 0 and a z score of -1?*
40. *Why are percentiles different from z scores?*
41. *Why do we convert z scores to T scores?*
42. *Convert the z scores calculated in Study Question 38 (i.e., +1.5, +1.0, +0.5, 0, -1.0, and -1.5) to T scores which have a mean of 50 and an S of 10.*

Summary
In this section the normal curve was discussed as it is used in testing. The deviation or z score was presented, and methods of using means other than zero were also presented. The difference between ordinally-scaled data, i.e., percentiles, and intervally-scaled data, i.e., deviation scores, was shown.

F. CORRELATION

In a previous section we presented the results of a test which was administered to a group of students. These results are given again in Figure 40, column 2, and the z scores are given in column 3. The mean of this test was 4, and the standard deviation was 2.

(1) Student's Name	(2) Raw Score First Test	(3) z Score First Test	(4) Raw Score Second Test	(5) z Score Second Test
Joe	7	+1.5	6	+1.0
Jane	6	+1.0	7	+1.5
Jim	5	+0.5	5	+0.5
Joan	4	0	1	-1.5
Jack	3	-0.5	4	0
Jill	2	-1.0	3	-0.5
John	1	-1.5	2	-1.0
	$M = 4; S = 2$		$M = 4; S = 2$	

Fig. 40. Scores for Seven Students on Two Tests

A second test was administered to this same group of students, and their raw scores on this test are given in the fourth column of the table. When the scores were added and the mean was calculated, it was found that the mean again was 4. In calculating the standard deviation, it was also discovered that this again was 2. The last column represents the computation of the z scores for this second test.

It would be nice if we had a way to express the relationship between these two sets of scores so that we could communicate this relationship to others. We might first want to graph the scores. We could represent one set along a horizontal axis and the other set along a vertical axis as illustrated in Figure 41.

Each point marked by an "x" represents an individual's score on both tests, and his or her name has been written beside the point to make this clear. For example, Joe scored a z score of +1.5 on the first test and a z score of +1.0 on the second test, so his point is defined by this address. The other six points were graphed in the same way. It is difficult to see a relationship

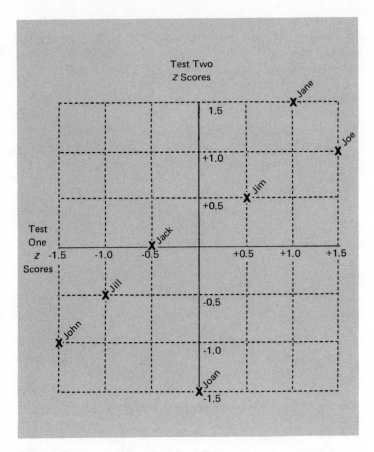

Fig. 41. Graph of *z* Scores for Two Tests

between these points because we do not have a large number
of people measured by our two tests. Increasing the number
of people measured by both tests might give us the graph
in Figure 42.

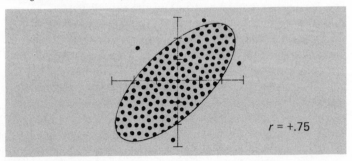

Fig. 42. Graph of the Scores of Two Tests, *r* = +.75

42

It appears that these points are scattering as indicated by the ellipse, which has only a few points outside the curve. This certainly tells us something about the relationship between the two tests, and this is quite different from another situation which has been graphed in Figure 43.

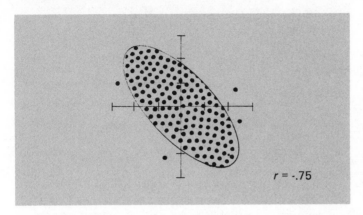

Fig. 43. Graph of the Scores of Another Two Tests, r = -.75

And this is quite different from the graph drawn in Figure 44.

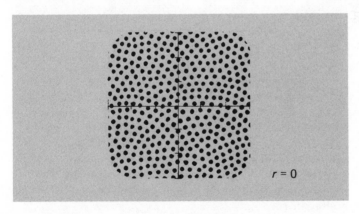

Fig. 44. Graph of the Scores on Two Tests, r = 0

It is desirable to have a number (i.e., a single index) to express the relationship between two sets of measures so that we do not have to draw a graph. The procedures for computing this index are illustrated in Figure 45. Using the original data from Figure 40, we first multiply our z scores together and obtain the products presented in column 4 of Figure 45.

43

Student's Name	z Score First Test	z Score Second Test	z_1z_2
Joe	+1.5	+1.0	1.50
Jane	+1.0	+1.5	1.50
Jim	+0.5	+0.5	0.25
Joan	0	-1.5	0
Jack	-0.5	0	0
Jill	-1.0	-0.5	0.50
John	-1.5	-1.0	1.50
			$\Sigma z_1z_2 = 5.25$

Fig. 45. Multiplying the z Scores

Next, we add the products to obtain a single number, i.e., 5.25. While this number is an index to the relationship between these two sets of data, this index is influenced by the number of people involved. To obtain a number which is *not* influenced in this way, we simply divide by N, the number of students involved. This has been done in Figure 46.

$$\text{Index 1} = \Sigma z_1z_2 = 5.25$$

$$\text{Index 2} = \frac{\Sigma z_1z_2}{N} = \frac{5.25}{7} = 0.75$$

Fig. 46. Indices of Relationship Between Two Tests

Now, if we wanted to write symbolically what we have done, we could write it as a formula. This would give us the formula in Figure 47 for the Pearson Product-Moment correlation coefficient, r.

$$r = \frac{\Sigma z_x z_y}{N}$$

Fig. 47. Formula for the Pearson Product-Moment Correlation Coefficient (r).

44

In this formula r is the coefficient of correlation, $\Sigma z_x z_y$ indicates that we have added the results of our multiplication of the z scores on two tests, and N is the number of cases. Notice how much more convenient it is to have a single index number to represent the graphing of these data.

The values of their correlation coefficients (r) have been written on the other graphs in Figures 42–44. Notice that a negative correlation coefficient with the same value as a positive correlation coefficient indicates the same degree of relationship between two measures except that the relationship is in the opposite direction (see Figures 42 and 43). A negative relationship exists if the student who scores high on one test scores low on the other test. If we had perfect agreement between the two measures ($r = 1.00$), all of our points would fall in a straight line. When the correlation is zero, there is *no* apparent relationship between the two measures, and the points form a shape that looks like a circle (Figure 44).

Study Questions:
43. *What is a correlation coefficient?*
44. *Before we can compute a correlation coefficient what data must we have?*
45. *What correlation coefficient represents perfect agreement between two sets of measures?*
46. *What does a negative correlation coefficient indicate?*
47. *What does a zero correlation coefficient indicate?*
48. *Using the z score method, compute the correlation for the two sets of test scores given below:*

(1) Student's Name	(2) z Score First Test	(3) z Score Second Test	(4) $z_1 z_2$
Avanell	1.5	0	_____
Andy	1.0	1.0	_____
Alvin	0.5	−1.5	_____
Arlene	0	0.5	_____
Ada	−0.5	1.5	_____
Alec	−1.0	−1.5	_____
Ann	−1.5	−1.0	_____

49. *Sum column 4:* $\Sigma z_1 z_2$ _____
50. *N =* _____
51. $r = \dfrac{\Sigma z_1 z_2}{N}$ = _____

It is not always convenient to calculate the correlation coefficient using the z-score method. A raw-score method is sometimes used. The formula presented in Figure 48 applies in such cases.

$$r = \frac{N\Sigma XY - \Sigma X\Sigma Y}{\sqrt{N\Sigma X^2 - (\Sigma X)^2} \ \sqrt{N\Sigma Y^2 - (\Sigma Y)^2}}$$

Fig. 48. Raw Score Formula for Computing r

In this formula, N is the number of people involved; ΣXY is the summation of the raw scores on one test multiplied by the raw scores on the other test; ΣX is the summation of the raw scores on one test; ΣY is the summation of the raw scores on the other test; ΣX^2 is the summation of the raw scores squared on one test; and ΣY^2 is the summation of the raw scores squared on the other test.

Using this formula, the correlation for the data given in Figure 45 has been computed in Figure 49. Notice that we obtained exactly the same results as in Figure 46.

Study Questions:
52. *Why would we find it inconvenient to always use the z-score formula?*
53. *To use the raw score formula we must calculate several pieces of information from our raw scores. If X represents the raw score on one test and Y represents the raw score on another test, tell how you would calculate the following:*
   a. ΣX
   b. ΣXY
   c. ΣY^2

Summary
The method of computing the Pearson Product-Moment coefficient r was presented and illustrated in this section. This coefficient was first computed using the z score method, and then computed using the raw score method. A graphing technique to demonstrate the relationship between these two variables was also given.

Name	Test 1 Score X	Test 2 Score Y	X^2	Y^2	XY
Joe	7	6	49	36	42
Jane	6	7	36	49	42
Jim	5	5	25	25	25
Joan	4	1	16	1	4
Jack	3	4	9	16	12
Jill	2	3	4	9	6
John	1	2	1	4	2
	$\Sigma X = 28$	$\Sigma Y = 28$	$\Sigma Y^2 = 140$	$\Sigma X^2 = 140$	$\Sigma XY = 133$

$$r = \frac{N\Sigma XY - \Sigma X \Sigma Y}{\sqrt{N\Sigma X^2 - (\Sigma X)^2}\ \sqrt{N\Sigma Y^2 - (\Sigma Y)^2}}$$

$$= \frac{7(133) - (28)\,(28)}{\sqrt{7(140) - (28)^2}\ \sqrt{7(140) - (28)^2}}$$

$$= \frac{931 - 784}{\sqrt{980 - 784}\ \sqrt{980 - 784}}$$

$$= \frac{147}{\sqrt{196}\ \sqrt{196}}$$

$$= \frac{147}{196}$$

$$r = 0.75$$

Fig. 49. Computing r Using the Raw Score Formula

G. RELIABILITY

Reliability is defined as the consistency or stability of a test. Let us assume that we gave the same test to an individual over and over, say eleven times, and then graphed his scores. We would find that the scores would look something like the illustration in Figure 50.

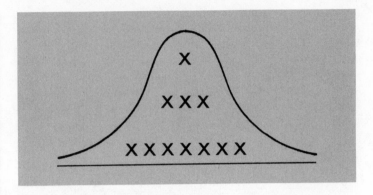

Fig. 50. Eleven Scores for One Individual on the Same Test

As additional scores are added, this distribution approaches the normal curve. Remember that this is one individual's test scores, and he was given the same test eleven times.

It is not practical to test the same individual with the same test over and over again to determine the stability of the score, primarily because he would probably become very uncooperative and refuse to keep taking the test. We have several statistical methods for *estimating* the stability of the scores, however. These methods of assessing reliability include test-retest, comparable-forms, and split-half techniques.

Test-Retest Reliability

The *test-retest reliability* technique involves administering a test to a group of students, waiting a short period of time, and then administering the test to them again. In using all correlation techniques, it is necessary that each individual have two test scores. These scores are then correlated, and an index of reliability is determined. It should be remembered with test-retest reliability, however, that *taking the first test might have changed the individuals* by making them more sensitive to the questions the second time the test was administered. The test-retest method, therefore, is most suitable to those situations when the characteristics being tested do not ordinarily change in the interval between the testing.

Comparable-Forms Reliability

Comparable-forms reliability is determined by administering one form of the test and then immediately administering a comparable or alternate form which is supposedly measuring the same thing as the first form measured.

Split-Half Reliability

The problem of the time lag between the two successive testings is overcome by the *split-half* technique. Basically, this involves administering one test and deriving two scores from it. First, the odd-numbered items are scored, and then the even-numbered items are scored, so that every student has **two scores** for the one administration of the test. As in previous examples, these two scores are correlated to obtain a measure of reliability. This type of reliability is sometimes referred to as "odd-even" reliability; however, the term "split-half" is in more general use.

Since half a test does not measure the characteristic as accurately as the complete test does, a statistical correction is usually made to overcome the problem of a shorter test. This is called the *Spearman-Brown Prophecy Formula* and is given in Figure 51.

$$r_{xx} = \frac{2r_{12}}{1 + r_{12}}$$

Fig. 51. The Spearman-Brown Prophecy Formula

In this formula, r_{xx} is the corrected reliability coefficient, and r_{12} is the original (uncorrected) correlation between the two halves of the test. This technique is used and reported in many standardized test manuals.

If the uncorrected correlation between two halves of a test is .75, we would use the Spearman-Brown Prophecy Formula as shown in Figure 52. Our corrected correlation would be .86, and this would be reported as the reliability of the test. The formula increases the size of the correlation to correct for the decrease in correlation when we divided the test into two shorter parts.

$$r = \frac{2(.75)}{1 + (.75)}$$

$$= \frac{1.50}{1.75}$$

$$= .857 = .86$$

Fig. 52. Computing the Spearman-Brown Correction

Study Questions:

54. *What would happen to an individual's score if he took the same test over, and over, and over?*
55. *What is test-retest reliability?*
56. *What is comparable-forms reliability?*
57. *What is split-half reliability?*
58. *What problems does the split-half reliability technique overcome?*
59. *A correlation of .80 was obtained through the split-half reliability technique. What corrected reliability would be reported?*

The Standard Error of Measurement

As we have already seen, the test scores of an individual fluctuate from testing to testing. If we made a distribution of these scores, and if we assumed that the middle of this distribution was the *true* score of an individual, it would be necessary to know the size of the fluctuation before we would be able to make accurate statements about the possible range of the test scores. It seems most appropriate to measure this in a standard deviation type of unit called the *standard error of measurement*. The formula for the standard error of measurement is given in Figure 53.

$$S_M = S_x \sqrt{1 - r_{xx}}$$

Fig. 53. Formula for the Standard Error of Measurement

In this formula, S_M is the standard error of measurement of the test, r_{xx} is the reliability of the test, and S_x is the standard deviation of the test.

Assume that the score a student obtains on any one test is most likely close to his "true" score; however, his scores on repeated testings will vary around or deviate from this "true" score in units like the normal distribution that we have discussed previously. The size of the deviation units is *determined by the standard error of measurement*. If the reliability were one, the standard error of measurement would be zero. This is understandable if you realize that with a correlation of one you have *no* error in the test score — that is, the exact same score will be obtained each time the individual takes the test. If the reliability were zero, the standard error of measurement is equal to the standard deviation of the test which was given. The higher the correlation, i.e., the closer to one, the smaller the standard error of measurement. The computation of the standard error of measurement is illustrated in Figure 54.

$$S_x = 2$$

$$r_{xx} = 0.75$$

$$S_M = S_x \sqrt{1 - r_{xx}}$$

$$= 2\sqrt{1 - 0.75}$$

$$= 2\sqrt{.25}$$

$$= 2(.5)$$

$$= 1.0$$

Fig. 54. Computation of the Standard Error of Measurement

Study Questions:
60. *What information does the standard error of measurement give us?*
61. *If a test had a reliability coefficient of .84 and a standard deviation of 3, what would the standard error of measurement be?*
62. *If the standard error of measurement for a standardized test is 2 and John obtained a score of 50, what are his chances of obtaining scores of 52 or higher if he took the test again? What are his chances of obtaining scores of 54 or higher?*

Summary

In this section, techniques for estimating the reliability or consistency of a test were discussed. These result in a correlation coefficient which gives us an index of the agreement between two sets of scores. Several methods of obtaining these two sets of scores were discussed, as well as the various kinds of coefficients: test-retest, comparable-forms, and split-half reliability with correction by the Spearman-Brown Prophecy Formula. The "true score" was also discussed, and the measure of variation around the true score was given as the standard error of measurement.

H. VALIDITY

Validity is defined as the degree to which the test measures what it is supposed to measure. It is sometimes very difficult to determine the validity of a test, and this becomes a complex task for testing specialists. The important question is: Does the test measure what it proposes to measure?

A test may have high reliability without having validity. For example, if we were measuring the distance a person could spit, we might well find that we have a highly reliable measure. However, to say that this is a measure of an individual's intelligence would be a very questionable procedure.

The American Psychological Association recommends that the concept of validity be divided into three types: construct, content, and criterion-related validity. Criterion-related validity is subdivided into two types: predictive and concurrent validity.

The Pearson Product-Moment Correlation is used as the coefficient of validity. We must, therefore, have two sets of measures — one set being the scores on the test which we are trying to validate. The other is the *criterion score*, which is another measure of the attribute which the test is proposing to measure. We therefore obtain a correlation between two measures — the test score and the criterion score. Our first problem in establishing validity, then, is to determine the criterion.

Criterion-Related Validity

Consider for a moment the problem of succeeding in college. The best method for measuring success in college might be the grade-point average at the end of an individual's college studies; but suppose that we wanted to predict an individual's college success *before* he entered college. We could save the individual time, effort, and money if we could advise him accurately as to his chances of success in college. Could we construct a test which would predict an individual's success in college? Yes, we probably could develop such a test, but how could we establish the validity of our measure?

To validate this test, we could give it to all students entering college. When they completed college, the test scores could be correlated with the criterion score — their academic grade-point average. Validation studies of this type are referred to as criterion-related validity, or more precisely, predictive validity. *Predictive validity* asks how well a test predicts a future event.

Concurrent validity is the second type of criterion-related validity and is similar to predictive validity except that the two measures are taken at the *same* time. In a concurrent validity study, the test must also be administered, but this time the criterion measure is obtained at the same time. Thus, if we administered our test to the seniors of the graduating class of our college, and correlated the results of their test with their grade-point average, we would call this concurrent validation. Figure 55 illustrates the difference between predictive validity and concurrent validity.

CRITERION-RELATED VALIDITY

Predictive Validity		Concurrent Validity	
Test Score	Criterion Score	Test Score	Criterion Score
Score on test administered at the beginning of the Freshman year	CORRELATED WITH	Grade-point average at the end of college studies	Score on test administered at the end of college studies	CORRELATED WITH	Grade-point average at the end of college studies

Fig. 55. Comparison of Predictive and Concurrent Validity

Content Validity

Validity studies often attempt to assess how well the test samples the type of behavior which it is designed to measure. This is called *content* or *face validity.* In this case, the problem with which we are concerned is the type and quality of the items included in the test. The question becomes: How well did this test cover the area which we are attempting to measure? This is usually not assessed with correlation techniques, but it is an important question which should be discussed in every test manual. The objectives of the test should be stated, and the rationale for using the items which form the content should be explained.

Construct Validity

The assessment of *construct validity* is somewhat more abstract and deals with the theory of testing and test construction. Let us take an example and develop it in detail.

Suppose we wanted to test "anxiety." Obviously, there is no way of assessing anxiety directly. Our first step in developing a test of anxiety would be to state our definition of the construct "anxiety." Suppose we define anxiety as a fear to which we cannot assign an object. (For example, if we are afraid of a snake, this is a fear; but if we are just afraid in general, this is an anxiety.) With this construct, then, we might include as one item on our test: "Are you sometimes afraid for no apparent reason?"

Several considerations become important with construct validity: How well does the test author state and operationally define the construct the test is attempting to measure? Can the test items be logically related to the operational definition of the construct as proposed by the author? And, using the author's definition of the construct, can empirically-testable hypotheses be developed?

Specialists in testing and measurement design research to measure construct validity. For example, if we wanted to test how adequately our test measures anxiety, we might hypothesize that when individuals who have demonstrated high achievement in school are put into a situation which threatens their concept of themselves as high achievers, their anxiety will increase.

We would now design situations where we could expect different levels of anxiety in order to test the hypothesis that individuals tested in a high-anxiety situation will score higher on our test than individuals who were tested in a low-anxiety situation. Figure 56 illustrates two such situations we might design.

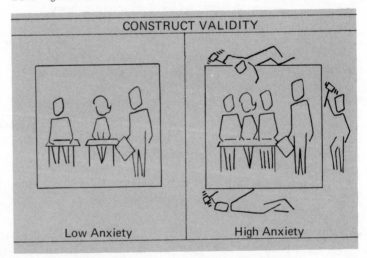

CONSTRUCT VALIDITY

Low Anxiety

High Anxiety

Fig. 56. Situations Designed to Test Construction of an "Anxiety" Test

First we might administer the test to a group on a pleasant, cool day, with no known threat present, and where the tester was pleasant and told the individuals that the results of the test had no meaning except for research. Then we would want to test a comparable group on a hot, humid day — when carpenters are pounding in the next room with hammers, and where the tester comes in and grouchily tells the group that their test results will determine whether or not they can continue in their present positions. These two types of testing situations should produce a difference in the test scores if the test measures the construct that it proposes to measure, i.e., anxiety, as it is defined in this case.

Although construct validity presents a difficult problem, the test manuals should define the construct being tested and the validation studies which have been done to support it.

Study Questions:
63. Define validity.
64. What is concurrent validity?
65. What is predictive validity?
66. What is content validity?
67. What is construct validity?

Summary

In this final section, the various methods of establishing the validity of a test were discussed. Predictive validity examines the question of the test's ability to forecast (or predict) success in a future endeavor. Concurrent validity is similar, but it is a correlation between the test score and a criterion measure assessed or obtained at the same time. Content validity assesses the purpose of the measure and how well the test items relate to this purpose. In construct validity, a hypothesized construct is proposed, and research is designed to measure how adequately the test measures the construct.

part 2
using
test
results

A. ASSIGNMENTS

The following assignments are suggested to direct your learning of the materials presented in Part II. Also, the test in Appendix C may help you apply Part I and Part II to the understanding and use of test data.

1. Consider a situation where you are, or might be, responsible for choosing a test. Describe your procedure for making a decision (outline only).

2. a. Construct a five-item test over Part II of this manual.

   b. What level of measurement or scale is your test?

   c. How do you report (accurately) a score derived from your test?

   d. How could you compare this score with another test score?

3. Use the outline for evaluating tests in Section D to evaluate four tests: an interest inventory, a personality test, an achievement test, and an ability test. If possible, evaluate tests that you might give or tests your school uses. Follow the outline. If answers are not available for some parts of the outline, please indicate this.

4. a. Make a test interpretation form for a test you have used or plan to use with students — see Figure 67 for an example. Use verbal descriptions as well as stanines.

   b. Role-play the interpretation of the test with your peers. (Use the Summary of Self-Estimate Test Interpretation Procedures in Section H.)

   c. What was your evaluation of the test interpretation procedures?

5. Try out the test interpretation procedures with several students, using several different types of tests, and with children of different age levels. Work with individuals or small groups until you are comfortable enough with the procedures to move to a larger group.

6. Try out the same test interpretation procedures with parents and teachers, that is, have a parent or both parents (or a teacher) estimate how they think the child scored on a test, and proceed as usual. With interest surveys, it might be interesting to compare the father's, mother's, and child's profile of estimated scores.

7. Questions to consider:

a. What are four ways test results may be used in your school or agency?

b. How does one decide *what* and *how many* tests to administer?

c. Why are raw scores considered "inaccurate" when test results are being interpreted?

d. Do you think schools and colleges should discontinue grades? What are some alternatives to grades?

e. How refined are our instruments for measuring performance? What kinds of errors do we make in expressing scores obtained from the use of these instruments?

f. (1) What are the levels or scales of measurement formulated by Stevens?

(2) What are the arithmetic limitations of each?

(3) Give examples of uses you make of each scale.

g. What do you need to know about a test before you administer it?

h. Define:

(1) validity

(2) reliability

(3) standard error of measurement

i. A test has a standard deviation (S) of 12 and a reliability coefficient (r) of .90.

(1) Compute the standard error of measurement (S_M) using the formula $S_M = S \sqrt{1 - r}.$

(2) Estimate the S_M using Figure 62.

j. What do we mean when we say a test is "standardized"?

k. (1) What formula is used to convert a raw score to a standard z score?

(2) What information is needed to compare scores from different tests using the z score?

l. (1) How is the student *involved* in the test interpretation procedures described in this manual?

(2) How long would it take to interpret a test in this manner to an individual? To a group?

m. What is the main disadvantage of using percentile ranks for reporting test scores?

n. According to this manual, what is the most *effective* and *efficient* way to report test scores?

B. USING TEST RESULTS

Whether teacher-made or standardized, any test that is administered should be useful in making an educational decision. Otherwise it is a waste of time and money. And while there may be some few exceptions, we basically agree with those who contend that test data should be interpreted to the one who took the test.

Using Test Data in Making Educational Decisions

Test data are used to make administrative and instructional decisions that affect individuals and groups, and data are used by the individual to make personal decisions. If the teacher or others use test data to make a decision relevant to grouping or curriculum modification, we might call these administrative decisions. If the data are used to plan units, individual instruction, or remediation, we might call these instructional decisions. When the teacher or counselor interprets the test score to the individual, and this information is used by that individual as part of the data in the decision-making process, then we could logically categorize this as a guidance use of tests.

Research is a fourth use of test data which may be the planned outcome of testing. Research may not permit interpretation of the test scores to the individual who took the test, but the individual should be made aware of the purpose of testing, and his permission should be obtained prior to administering the test. We feel this would eliminate much of the frustration and criticism of testing, and would also ensure the right to privacy for the individual concerned.

Fig. 57. Committee May Recommend a Testing Program

The objectives of the testing program will, of course, determine the tests which will be administered and the people who will be concerned with the individual and group data. Generally, a committee will assist in formulating the objectives and recommending the types of tests which should comprise the standardized testing program.

C. THE PROBLEMS OF REPORTING PERFORMANCE

How specific or accurate can we be in measuring factors concerning people? One of our greatest errors in measurement in the area of social sciences is assuming more accuracy than the measuring instrument warrants and then applying inappropriate computations to the data.

Degrees of Refinement in Using Test Data

You will recall from Part I that at best our test data reach the level of interval scaling, which has an agreed-upon zero point, but that that zero point does not mean or imply the absence of the factor being considered. Thus, we cannot report standardized-test data with the degree of refinement that John can report the difference in the amount of money he and Sam possess in Figure 58. (See also Figure 61.)

Fig. 58. Expressing Amounts Appropriately

How specific can we be when we express differences and amounts? That depends upon the measuring instrument used. In Figure 58, Sam and John are referring to money which is measured in agreed-upon units, i.e., on a ratio scale; thus, John can express the amount of money he has in *exact* terms, and it is appropriate for him to use multiplication. Would this be true if they were talking about ability?

For example, which is the most *accurate* statement?

1. "He has an IQ of 103."
2. "According to this test, he has average ability."
3. "On this measure of aptitude — which measures verbal and mathematical ability — he scored about like the average student for his age and grade level."

The first statement is often heard, but it is inaccurate. First, to interpret scores using specific score values *implies* greater accuracy than the test can possibly yield. Also, we do not know how this score compares with other possible scores, and we do not know how to estimate the error band.

The second statement is more accurate than the first, but it still implies greater accuracy than the test data warrant. True, the test interpretation category of "average" is broad, but *ability* is a general factor or construct which most tests are too limited to measure accurately. Thus, to define the *factors* measured by the test, and to indicate comparative performance, as in the third statement, is the most accurate. (See the discussion in Part I, under Construct Validity, for more information concerning this important point.)

The degree of refinement in measurement may be broadly categorized as follows:

1. *Two-way classification* is the broadest and most general level of measurement. Interestingly enough, measurement has become quite a popular issue on the college campus and has been the subject of some student demands. Many students and faculty members feel that the two-way classification of Pass-Fail is adequate for most purposes of evaluation, is more accurate than letter grades, and respects the rights of the individual by evaluating him in terms of outside criteria rather than forcing competition for letter grades, such as A, B, C, D, and F.

Fig. 59. Evaluation as an Issue in Recent Student Demonstrations

2. *Qualitatively-described degrees* are the next level of refinement in measurement. In our everyday conversation we make use of this: We say such things as "average ability," "slow learners," "bright," and "very bright." We distinguish between degrees in such terms as "attractive," "very pretty," "beautiful," etc. Of course, one problem with this type of measurement is the vagueness of the terms and the potential differences in meaning of the words for the individuals with whom we are attempting to communicate.

3. *Rank in group* is the next level of refinement in measurement. This system allows us to rank students from most to least able on a series of tasks which are scored by relatively uniform standards. This procedure suffers from the limitation that there is not an established level of performance, and the differences in ability or distances between individuals may not be equal. For example, on a hypothetical test involving thirty tasks, the students and the number of tasks completed without error are shown in Figure 60.

Student	Number of Items Completed	Rank in Group
Sally	30	1
John	29	2
Earle	25	3
Patty	24	4
Anne	23	5
Fred	22	6
Julia	15	7
Juanita	14	8

Fig. 60. Ranking of Students According to Performance on a Thirty-Item Test

An examination of Figure 60 shows the uneven distances between ranks. Sally completed all items correctly and only one item more than John, who ranked second; whereas Earle, ranked third, completed five items fewer than Sally. Again, Fred ranked sixth with 22 items correct, but Julia was seventh with only 15 items correct. While the disadvantage of this type of measurement is obvious, we use it as the basis for much of our decision-making relative to grades and for reporting test scores when we convert the ranks to percentiles. The advantages of this type of measurement are that it is accepted by parents and it is convenient.

4. *Amount, expressed in uniform, established units*, is
our most refined level of measurement, but many variables do
not lend themselves to this method. Variables such as weight,
height, speed of response, money — as in Figure 58 — may be
expressed in uniform measurements; but intelligence, anxiety,
happiness, and similar constructs, are not expressed in agreed-
upon standard units.

Our first attempts at measuring intelligence were to measure skull size and shape, thus attempting to apply this level of
measurement. However, such procedures for measuring intelligence have long since been discarded.

Levels or Types of Scales

Understanding human behavior and interpreting that behavior to others did not move into the realm of science until
we began to quantify description. Yet, as pointed out earlier,
we tend to assume more accuracy than we should when we
assign numbers, and we also tend to assume that all of the operations of elementary arithmetic — addition, subtraction, multiplication, and division — and all statistical procedures are appli-
cable to all levels or types of measurement. These assumptions
are not true and result in many errors in our conclusions drawn
from analysis of data.

S. S. Stevens[1] formulated four levels or scales of measurement, or four possible ways of assigning numerals. Each level or
scale has arithmetic rules and restrictions, and each has certain
statistical procedures which are appropriate to it. These scales
correspond to, but are somewhat different from, the degrees of
refinement of measurement discussed earlier.

The first or lowest level of measurement is the *nominal
scale.* This is nothing more than counting or numbering and may
be applied to individuals, as when assigning numbers to football
players, or to groups, as when assigning a code number to females
and a different code number to males. The only arithmetic operation appropriate to this type of scale is counting. For example,
the Dean may count the number of applicants meeting the entrance requirements and the number of applicants failing to meet
the requirements. The only statistical techniques appropriate for
nominal scales are those based on counting.

Next is the *ordinal scale*, where the numbers indicate a rank
in a group. For an example of this scale, see Figure 60. We use

---

[1] Stevens, S. S. *Handbook of Experimental Psychology,*
New York: Wiley, 1951.

Refinement in Measurement	Illustration (General)	Illustration (School)	Limitation
Two-way Classification	1 2	ADMISSION REPORT ACT x 2 (G)=6 GPA x D(A)=38 *MINORITY (NO) REJE ACT OR ASG P	Broad categories provide little information
Qualitatively-Described	Transportation Good Better Best	PERMANENT RECORD CHECK FOR EACH STUDENT ATTITUDE 1 NEATNESS 2 BEHAVIOR 1 PROMPTNESS 3	Meaning of words not clear or specific
Rank		GRADES ON TEST 100 . . . . . 1 98 . . . . . 2 97 . . . . . 3 90 . . . . . 3 85 . . . . . 3 80 . . . . . 1 74 4	Distance between intervals not equal
Amount in Standard Units	50 lbs. 100 lbs. 50 100	TYPING TEST WPM=60 (corrected for errors) 20(errors)=WPM 5	Not applicable to most psychological constructs

Fig. 61. Degrees of Refinement in Measurement

the ordinal scale in computing percentile scores, and we can apply statistical techniques appropriate to nominal data and to the interpretation of "greater than" or "less than." For example, a teacher may report that a certain student ranked second on a spelling test, but we do not know how much better the best speller was, nor how much better the second speller was than the third best. The only arithmetic operation appropriate to ordinal level data is counting or numbering. The distances between these ordinal numbers are unequal (see Figure 60 to verify this); therefore, we cannot add, subtract, multiply, or divide ordinal level data.

The *interval scale* is the next level identified by Stevens. The interval scale provides *equal distances between intervals,* but the zero point is not known. For example, a zero obtained by a student on an achievement test does not mean the absence of all information. The zero point is simply an agreed-upon point. In a similar fashion, we could say that at zero Fahrenheit there is still warmth. The only arithmetic operations appropriate to interval level data are addition and subtraction, and the statistical techniques appropriate are those already indicated for nominal and ordinal data and those appropriate to addition and subtraction.

The *ratio scale* is the fourth and highest level of measurement. All arithmetic operations and all statistical techniques are appropriate to ratio scales. As the name implies, ratio data may be expressed as a ratio; thus multiplication and division, as well as addition and subtraction, are appropriate. The ratio scale has all of the characteristics of the interval scale, plus the important characteristic that the *zero point is known*. Thus, when we express weight, height, distance, and similar measures, we are using ratio scales (see Figure 58 as an illustration). Unfortunately, we cannot use a ratio scale when we attempt to measure most psychological constructs. When we measure such factors as reaction time or words per minute we employ a ratio scale; however, constructs such as ability or interest are measured on interval scales (the *absence* of the construct is not even implied).

If we remember the degrees of refinement of the psychological measurement and the arithmetic limitations when interpreting test data obtained from our psychological instruments, then we can use the data effectively. If we treat all data alike, ignoring the limitations discussed above, then the test data can and probably will contribute to errors in decision-making.

D. EVALUATING TESTS

Sometimes you may wish to be able to select appropriate tests for certain purposes, and at other times you may wish to evaluate tests already in use. What do you look for when evaluating tests? We would suggest applying the following considerations to each instrument considered.

Choosing a Test

Tests should not be chosen for reasons of prominence and popularity — although these are frequently the only reasons outdated and out-moded tests continue to be used. Neither should tests be discarded simply because of the date of publication; instead, their value should be judged in comparison to the more recent instruments designed to serve the same function. Length of testing time, ease of scoring, face validity, or similar necessary, but insufficient, reasons are often given for choosing a test. Tests should be selected according to a specific set of criteria to prevent relatively superficial factors from exerting too great an influence.

A test certainly cannot reveal information not contained in the questions. This fact is so obvious that its importance may be overlooked in test selection. A test should never be chosen on the basis of its reputation alone, and its content should not be judged from the title alone. Only from an examination of the *items and rationale* of the test can the examiner determine the validity of a test to yield the information he is seeking to obtain.

A procedure for a systematic and thorough examination of tests is given in the following outline. We recommend that you apply *each* question to every test which is being considered for use.

Outline for Evaluating a Test

1. Name of test

2. What construct or quality is this test designed to measure?

3. What is your purpose for evaluating the test?

4. Practical features

   a. Time considerations

      (1) Time required to administer total test

      (2) Could the time requirements be handled in your situation?

      (3) Time required to score

      (4) Who could score the test in your situation?

b. Financial considerations
   (1) Cost of test booklets
   (2) Cost of answer sheets
   (3) Cost of machine scoring per student
   (4) Cost of other materials (list)
c. General considerations
   (1) Are the directions for administering clear?
   (2) Are the directions for scoring clear?
   (3) Are the directions for interpreting scores clear?
   (4) Are answer sheets appropriate for age and ability level of students?
   (5) What training is required to administer the test?
   (6) Are the test items up-to-date?
   (7) Are the norms up-to-date?

5. Test items
   a. How many items are included in the test?
   b. What is the reading level?
   c. How were the test items chosen by the author?
   d. Do the test items seem logical (to you) for the purpose for which they were chosen?

6. Reliability
   a. What evidence of reliability is given?
   b. How reliable is the measurement over time (i.e., reliability coefficient)?

7. Validity
   a. What evidence of validity is given?
   b. Which validity study provides the highest correlation coefficient?
   c. Which validity study provides the lowest correlation coefficient?

8. Norms
   a. What type of norms are provided?
   b. Are the procedures for collecting normative data described?
   c. Does the normative sample seem truly representative?
   d. Are the norms relevant for your purpose?

9. Reviews
   a. What are the general comments of the reviewers?
   b. What are the special strengths of the test?

    c. What are the special weaknesses of the test?

    d. What references did you use?

10. General Evaluation

    a. What is your general evaluation of the test?

    b. For what purpose and group would you recommend this test?

    c. What are some competing instruments which should be considered?

Sources of Information About Tests

Oscar Buros publishes reviews of tests in the *Mental Measurement Yearbook*, which appears approximately every five years. His efforts are directed at assisting individuals to make logical test choices and the best use of test data through knowledge of the strengths and limitations of the tests. Two or more experts discuss each test and provide a basis for judging its worth. Buros provides the best single source of information about tests. Technical journals and textbooks provide additional references.

E. VALIDITY

— Is this a good test? — How often have you heard or asked this question? Goodness *per se* is an inadequate standard for a test. A test is good — or valid — if it *meets the objective for which it is intended*. If a test serves its intended function well, then we would say it is *valid*. A test is chosen to answer a question about an individual or group and is validated in reference to its intended purpose.

Basically, there are three types of validity: *content, construct*, and *predictive*. (See Part I for a discussion of validity from a statistical viewpoint.) What are the purposes of these types of validity and how is each determined? An examination of the three types of validity will assist you in determining *whether a test is good for the purpose for which you are using it*.

Content Validity

Content validity is concerned with the content or subject matter covered by the test. Assessment of achievement and teacher-made tests is generally concerned with this type of validity. Since the purpose of this type of test is to measure the amount of material learned and/or behavior changed in a given unit, subject, or program, the achievement test provides an adequate sample of all possible items from which the test might be drawn.

Content validity is determined by comparing the test items and the content covered in the unit, subject, or program. Usually an outline of the material and the test items are compared to determine if the test items are *representative*, *adequate*, and *appropriate*.

Construct Validity

Construct validity is concerned with the measurement of psychological constructs or traits. The purpose of validating a test designed to measure a construct is to determine if in reality the quality being measured is the one which is sought.

An example of a construct or a trait we might want to measure is *aggression*. There are several ways we might support the notion that the test items do indeed measure the trait of aggression:

1. We might ask "experts," such as psychologists, juvenile delinquency counselors, teachers, etc., to rate the items comprising the test for their appropriateness for measuring the construct. (In this instance we assume the "experts" are accurate in their evaluation of the items.)

2. We might compare scores on the new instrument with scores obtained on an instrument which has gained acceptance as being valid for measuring the construct of aggression. (Of course, in this situation, our assumption is that the earlier test does indeed measure the desired construct.) One highly respected and accepted test of intelligence is the *Wechsler Adult Intelligence Scale* (WAIS), and thus most tests of intelligence (a psychological construct) are validated against the Wechsler test — supporting the "goodness" of the new test in this way.

3. We might compare scores of individuals who are assumed to rate high on the trait with individuals who are assumed to rate low on the trait. For example, scores obtained from certain prison inmates may be compared to scores obtained from priests. The test should yield scores that distinguish between the two groups. (Of course, we are assuming that the two comparison groups are in reality different relative to the trait being measured.)

4. Finally, we might experimentally induce a condition to enhance or strengthen the influence of the construct on the test behavior of the examinee. In our study of aggression, we could describe a threatening situation and then ask the examinee to respond to the questions as if he were experiencing

the threatening situation. Test scores obtained prior to and following the experiment should reflect the different situations. (We are, of course, assuming that the experiment does in reality influence the test behavior relevant to the construct under consideration.)

We would emphasize here that construct validity is specific to a group and/or situation. Thus, appropriate validity studies are crucial to accepting a test as measuring a trait for any given population or group.

Predictive Validity

Predictive validity is a more common type of validity and easily explained. An example of a test used for this purpose is an entrance examination given for admission into a particular college or school program. The grades obtained by the student are predicted on the basis of the test performance, and are validated by follow-up studies to determine how accurately the grades were predicted. (We assume, in this instance, that the ability reflected in the test performance is possessed prior to entering the program, and that it is of the nature required for success in the program.)

F. RELIABILITY

When we test, we sample behavior in an attempt to obtain an *estimate* of the individual's performance in a much larger number of possible situations. For example, if we would like to test a student's mathematical competencies, we do not ask all possible questions; instead, we choose a sample of items from the many possible items. We assume that to the extent the student is accurate in answering the items on the test, he will be accurate in answering the other items which were *not* asked on the test. If this assumption is to have merit, then the sample of behavior must be valid and the test must be *reliable* (i.e., consistent in measuring whatever it measures).

The degree of consistency of a measure obtained from a test is expressed as a reliability coefficient (r). The closer to 1.00 the correlation, the more consistent the test. For example, one way the reliability is determined is to give the same test twice, and the relationship of the scores obtained is compared. The degree of correspondence will fall somewhere between $\pm$ 1.00. (Part I discusses various ways to determine reliability.)

A test must be reliable to be valid; however, the converse is not true. Since such factors as guessing, speed, anxiety, etc., can cause some fluctuation in the responses on a test, we know we would not obtain the exact same score on a test if it were taken by the same individual on more than one occasion. Yet if the scores are not fairly similar, then we could put no confidence whatsoever in the instrument. Therefore, we do want to know how reliable the instrument is and how to estimate the amount of error for the obtained score. (See Part I, Reliability, for a discussion of these concepts from a statistical viewpoint.) We must know the degree of reliability before we can determine the standard error of measurement, i.e., the length of the band for the score.

Standard Error of Measurement

The standard error of measurement (S_M) is an estimate of the standard deviation for the scores that would be obtained from a series of measurements of the same individual (the band within which the obtained scores would fall). *It is this deviation of obtained scores that determines the length of the band for a test score.*

The *error* in the test is the *chance variation of the obtained scores* for one individual on the same test. The standard error of measurement is a function of both the reliability coefficient (*r*) and the standard deviation (*S*) of the test for the normative group. *As the reliability coefficient decreases and the standard deviation for the test scores increases, the standard error of measurement becomes greater.* (To verify this, see Figure 62.)

Figure 62 provides a table for estimating the standard error of measurement when the reliability coefficient and standard deviation are known. The table is based on the formula $S_M = S \sqrt{1-r}$.

For most purposes the result will be sufficiently accurate if the table is entered with the reliability and standard deviation values nearest those given in the test manuals. Also, for most purposes the number should be rounded to the nearest whole number. Thus, if the test's reliability is reported to be .87, with a standard deviation of 10.3, you would use the values .85 and 10, respectively, in Figure 62 to find the estimated standard error of 3.9 or 4 raw score points. (When computed from the original data, the standard error of measurement would be 3.7 or 4 raw score points.)

Standard Deviation S	Reliability Coefficient (r)						
	.95	.90	.85	.80	.75	.70	.65
	Numbers indicate raw score points for 1 S_M						
30	6.7	9.5	11.6	13.4	15.0	16.4	17.7
28	6.3	8.9	10.8	12.5	14.0	15.3	16.5
26	5.8	8.2	10.1	11.6	13.0	14.2	15.4
24	5.4	7.6	9.3	10.7	12.0	13.1	14.2
22	4.9	7.0	8.5	9.8	11.0	12.0	13.0
20	4.5	6.3	7.7	8.9	10.0	11.0	11.8
18	4.0	5.7	7.0	8.0	9.0	9.9	10.6
16	3.6	5.1	6.2	7.2	8.0	8.8	9.4
14	3.1	4.4	5.4	6.3	7.0	7.7	8.3
12	2.7	3.8	4.6	5.4	6.0	6.6	7.1
10	2.2	3.2	3.9	4.5	5.0	5.5	5.9
8	1.8	2.5	3.1	3.6	4.0	4.4	4.7
6	1.3	1.9	2.3	2.7	3.0	3.3	3.5
4	.9	1.3	1.5	1.8	2.0	2.2	2.4
2	.4	.6	.8	.9	1.0	1.1	1.2

Adapted from: *Test Service Bulletin No. 51.* The Psychological Corporation, December, 1965.

Fig. 62. Standard Errors of Measurement (S_M) for Given Values of the Reliability Coefficient (r) and the Standard Deviation (S)

Some test publishers provide the standard error of measurement as well as the reliability coefficients in the test manuals. However, determining the S_M is a relatively simple mathematical procedure requiring only the standard deviation for the appropriate norm group and the reliability coefficient. The formula is:

$$S_M = S \sqrt{1 - r}$$

Where: S_M = Standard error of measurement,
S = Standard deviation,
r = Reliability coefficient.

Suppose the test we are considering has a reported S of 10 and r of .60, the S_M for this test is:

$$S_M = S \sqrt{1 - r}$$
$$= 10 \sqrt{1 - .60}$$
$$= 10 \sqrt{.40}$$
$$= 10 \, (.63)$$
$$= 6.3, \text{ rounded} = 6$$

In this example we see that for this test the S_M is 6 raw-score points on each side of the obtained test score ($\pm 1\, S_M$); that is, a band extending 6 raw-score points on each side of the obtained score will include the "true" score (the score that would actually be obtained) two-thirds of the time (see Figure 63). We might say we can be 68 percent sure the "true" score will fall within this band. If we want to be more certain — 95 percent sure — that the band includes the "true" score, we would extend the band to include two standard-error units — in this case, 12 raw-score points — from the score ($\pm 2\, S_M$).

For classroom purposes the S_M may be rounded and/or the band may be approximated (such as one inch). Also, Figure 62 may be used for estimating the S_M for any score with enough accuracy for most classroom use of test results.

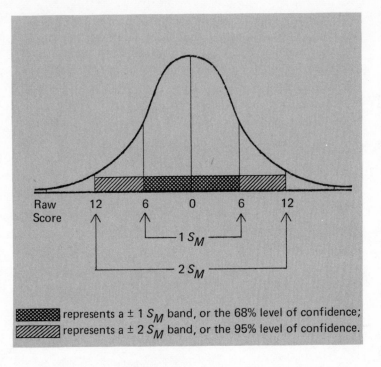

Raw Score

| | 12 | 6 | 0 | 6 | 12 |

$1 S_M$

$2 S_M$

▨ represents a ± 1 S_M band, or the 68% level of confidence;
▨ represents a ± 2 S_M band, or the 95% level of confidence.

Fig. 63. Distribution of Scores Obtained by One Individual on the Same Test

G. STANDARDIZATION

What makes a standardized test different from a teacher-made test? By definition, a standardized test is a measuring instrument which must be administered under prescribed conditions and scored in a predetermined manner. Also, the interpretation of data is in terms of a normative group drawn as a representative sample of a described population of a specific age or educational level. Thus, the purpose of a standardized test is to make it possible to compare and, in a sense, rank people in terms of the specific behaviors sampled, i.e., items asked on the test.

The first two of these characteristics are not too difficult to accomplish, even though numerous errors can be made because of carelessness. Choosing appropriate norms presents a more difficult problem.

Norms

Norms provide a yardstick with which a pupil's raw score can be compared. In the normative group, one-half of the group is below average and one-half is above average. "High" and "low" performances are in relation to the deviation (distance) of the raw score from the mean.*

One way to compare scores on a test is to convert the scores to standard or z scores and compare them to the norm (see Figure 38, Part I, for the z-score distribution). Example:

$$z = \frac{(X - M)}{S}$$

Where: X = raw score,
M = mean (average),
S = standard deviation for the test.

Now, let us compare Bill's score with his classmates' scores on a math test. Bill's score was 80, the mean for the group was 90, and the standard deviation was 20. Thus,

$$z = \frac{80 - 90}{20}$$
$$= \frac{-10}{20}$$
$$= -.5$$

In this example we can see that Bill scored one-half a standard deviation unit below the mean.

This method can be used to compare one student's scores on several tests (if the M and S are known for each), and to compare a student with a normative group. *The normative group must be appropriate to the age and/or grade level. We cannot equate scores on tests using different normative groups.*

If national norms are used, the sample should be *truly* representative of those with whom comparisons are to be made. Some of the factors that influence performance besides age and education are sex, socio-economic level, geographical region, and language spoken; therefore, these factors along with others should be considered in choosing the sample. Norms which are developed on the basis of convenience of location or accessibility of students are suspect. Local norms should be developed when possible.

---

*"Norms" should not be confused with "standards." Standards are established by stating a certain minimum score to be "acceptable" or "passing." For example, in many school systems the passing grade is set at 65 or 70, which may be obtained by *all* students.

People-in-general norms are seldom useful except for ability tests which yield IQ scores and for certain clinical situations. People-in-general norms may be misleading, in some instances, where the average for a group has no meaning for a person who must perform specific tasks. For example, the skills needed by one secretary for one firm might be limited to typing and filing; whereas the skills of secretaries in general might include shorthand, use of various machines, and answering the telephone.

Sometimes we find that the recommended normative group may not be appropriate for meaningful interpretations of test data. For example, math aptitude scores are usually lower for females than for males. A girl who is considering majoring in math, or is considering a career in which math aptitude is important, will probably be competing with males. In such situations, we have found it quite helpful to compare the girl's scores with scores obtained by males — which will be her reference group in making the decisions.

The test user is urged to try out interpretations of an individual's test score using a number of different normative groups, to get an idea of the wide range of meanings which may be applied.

H. INTERPRETING TEST SCORES

The test interpretation procedures recommended here are designed to solicit student *involvement* and, therefore, result in his "self" interpretation — the procedures allow the student to make the application of the information obtained from the test to his own plans, and to determine the appropriateness of the test results for making educational, vocational, and personal decisions.

Involving the Student — The Self-Estimate Procedure for Test Interpretation

First, the student should be involved in describing the test and deciding what it measures, and the student himself should determine the appropriateness of the data to the questions he would like answered. This procedure has the student estimate his test score prior to learning the obtained score; thus, it requires him to think through his usual performance in similar situations, and to compare his performance with other students of the same age and/or grade level (the normative group). While students tend to estimate scores with amazing accuracy, any discrepancy between his self-estimate and his actual performance usually stimulates discussion, allowing the teacher or counselor to clarify the information and thus prevent any misunderstanding or misinterpretation which might occur.

In the procedure described herein, the data are reported in terms of *bands* to insure a consideration of the standard error of measurement and significant differences between scores. Also, *no raw scores are used* — raw scores and percentile scores tend to imply greater accuracy and preciseness than are warranted. An example of the problems inherent in using numbers is seen when one examines the use of the concept of the intelligence quotient (IQ). Binet used the IQ as a shorthand method of indicating that the student's performance on a specific test or variable deviated from the mean (above or below) for the age group in general. The IQ summarized the formula ($CA/MA \times 100$) and implied a measurement error. However, with use the *intent* seems to have been forgotten; and the IQ — the quotient — has come to mean *an amount* of ability, or capacity. Thus, the warning against the use of numbers. The verbal descriptions used in this interpretation enhance the understanding of the meaning of the data which are reported as bands.

These procedures, i.e., using bands and verbal descriptions, are appropriate with individuals and large or small groups. Confidentiality is maintained in groups, since all data are handed to the individual in written form, and no individual data are revealed to the group. These procedures provide accurate information, yet prevent "over-interpretation," and take cognizance of the ethical considerations relevant to test data.

Involving Parents, Teachers, and Others

These procedures may be used with the elementary school child as well as with parents, teachers, or any other person interested in learning the performance of an individual on a test. With parents, we have found it useful to have them estimate how they think their child performed prior to providing them with the obtained scores. This makes discussion about scores and expectations much more meaningful, and it forces consideration of reality.

One additional advantage of these interpretation procedures is that the variables measured by the test are defined in written form, and the bands are reported in written form; thus, these materials may be taken home and discussed with the parents. Gradually, the anxiety about testing and score interpretation is lowered, and the test becomes a vehicle for "learning about oneself" rather than a weapon whereby the student is "judged" by others.

Summary of Procedures

A summary outline of the test interpretation procedures is presented as Figure 64, at the beginning of the discussion, to assist you in learning the technique, and as a convenient reference guide to keep before you while presenting data to students.

Summary of Self-Estimate Test Interpretation Procedures

1. Establish rapport.
2. Talk about the test itself (show booklet, items, etc.)
3. Find out how students felt when they took the test — was it a typical situation for the individual?
4. Help students understand the objectives or purposes of the test and some ways the data might be used.
5. Present the normal distribution.
6. Explain *average*, *low*, and *high* performance.
7. Explain the error in test scores.
8. Discuss the use of bands for interpreting test scores.
9. Have students estimate their scores.
10. Have students compare estimated performance with actual performance (band).
11. Help students apply the information to decisions they may make — educational and vocational.
12. Summarize.
13. Encourage further discussions with parents.
14. Invite students to make additional appointments.

Fig. 64. Test Interpretation Outline

Understanding the Test Interpretation Procedures

1. Establish rapport.

Don't use the beginning of a test interpretation session for small talk about such things as the last ball game. Basically, the student wants to learn his test scores, and if he has made an appointment to see you for this purpose — or if you have scheduled the session (group or individual) for this purpose — you may proceed immediately with the interpretations. To avoid the subject which is the real reason for the session may indicate a dread on your part, and this may be interpreted as "bad news" by the students. A simple greeting and something like "I believe we are here to discuss your performance on the Reading Development Test you took last week" is probably sufficient to establish good rapport. This kind of behavior is positive and is usually interpreted as friendly, helpful, and reassuring.

2. Talk about the test itself.

Help students recall what the test was like — show them the test booklet and sample items. Talk about when and where the test was taken and who administered it.

3. Ask, "How did you feel when you took the test?"

Talk about this. If for any reason you doubt the validity of a test (for example, suppose a student had to leave the room to receive an upsetting message during the test), then the data should be interpreted with that reservation in mind. When necessary, make arrangements for the student to take another form of the test.

Help students understand that the test should provide an estimate of their "typical" behavior. Discussion at this point prevents students from making excuses before learning how they scored — i.e., they decide at this point whether the testing situation was valid for them. *This also involves them in their first decision about the data* — to accept and to use the data, or not to accept and to ignore the data. Both behaviors are appropriate at times.

4. Ask, "Why do you think this test was chosen?" (if required by the school), or "Why did you choose this test?" (if requested by the student).

Talk about what scores the test yields, for example, reading comprehension and word recognition: What decisions can be or will be made on the basis of the data? How might the information be used in making decisions?

5. Ask, "What do we know about the test scores of the people who took this test and with whom your scores will be compared?" (Be specific about the normative group here: for example, "Your scores will be compared with those of all ninth-graders in West Virginia who have taken this test.")

Talk about such things as the normal distribution (most youngsters become familiar with this concept in about the third or fourth grade), explaining that this distribution represents every score from the lowest to the highest. (Draw the distribution as you talk or have one ready to present as you talk.)

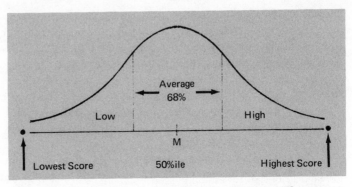

Fig. 65. Normal Distribution Representing Normative Group

6. Ask, "If you didn't know anything else about the way a person scored, where along the line (Figure 65) — from the lowest to the highest — would you guess the score would fall?"

They will probably "guess" average because most (i.e., two-thirds) of the scores fall within the average range. Explain that some scores (about 15%) fall above average and some scores (about 15%) fall below average.

7. Say, "Let's pretend you scored exactly in the middle (at the 50th percentile) of the distribution." (Illustrate by placing an X on that point of the distribution.) Ask, "If you took the same test again today, would you score in the same, exact place?"

The group will probably agree that their scores would not be the same because of such factors as "feeling great today," guessing differently — better or worse, remembering an answer, etc. (As they talk and give reasons, illustrate these fluctuations in the scores by adding X's as illustrated in Figure 66.)

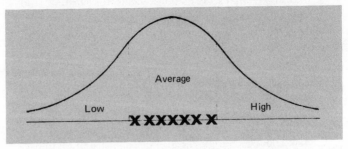

Fig. 66. Using X's to Illustrate Band

8. Discuss the use of bands for interpreting test scores.

Explain that since test scores obtained on successive testings vary somewhat, we have to estimate where the "true" score would probably fall. For this reason we use a *band* for reporting test data — and we can be 95 percent confident (this band includes $\pm 2\,S_M$) that the score would fall within this band. (Figure 66 illustrates a band which includes most of the test scores that would be obtained by one individual taking the same test on a number of occasions.)

9. Hand out the self-estimate form.

Ask each student to estimate (put an X) on the distribution about where he thinks he scored on each variable for the test. (The student's self-estimate form should provide the name of the test, a definition of the variables measured, and a representation of the normal distribution for estimating the test score, as in Figure 67). (Also, see Appendix E and Appendix F for examples of Self-Estimate Forms used for other tests.)

We would suggest that the numbers representing the stanines *not* be included on the form, but they are included here for clarification.

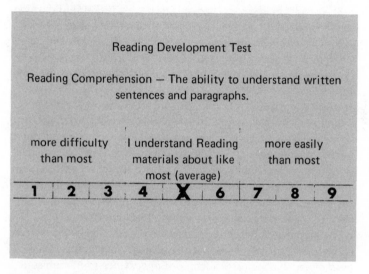

Fig. 67. Test Interpretation Form for Self-Estimate of Test Scores. X Indicates Student's Estimate of Score

10. After the student has estimated the test score, hand him another form with his own test results reported in the form of a band as in Figure 68. (The length of the band is determined by the S_M and may be estimated from Figure 62 if the standard deviation and reliability coefficient are known.)

Ask the students to compare their estimated scores and their obtained scores. Explain that the estimate is accurate if it falls anywhere within the band.

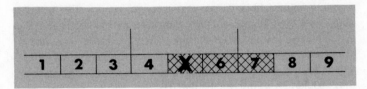

Fig. 68. Test Interpretation Form and Band Showing Student's
    Score and Student's Estimate

11. Ask, "How did you perform on the test? Did you perform about the way you expected to perform?"

Students tend to be amazingly accurate in their self-estimate
of test scores — this is borne out by research — and when the estimate and band are vastly different, we usually find one of two
reasons for the discrepancy: a. Either the student did not understand the definition of the variable, or b. The scoring and reporting
of the band was in error. Thus, this technique is useful in spotting
errors in reporting scores as well as serving as a counseling device.

One interesting example of a student's misunderstanding of
a definition was brought to our attention when we were using self-
estimate as a procedure in interpreting the *Edwards Personal Pref-
erence Schedule* (EPPS) to a college sophomore. The EPPS measures the importance of fifteen variables or needs. In the verbal
descriptions in the interpretation we used the word *need*, i.e.,
"Achievement — a need to succeed," etc. The self-estimates made
by one student were almost on the opposite ends of the distribution from the obtained scores. The scoring was checked, but no
error was found. As we pursued the interpretation with the student,
she said something to this effect: "But I don't understand why I
need (Achievement) when it is already real important to me!" She
was using the word *need* to mean something was *lacking*; whereas,
according to the test the opposite was true — a high score on a
need or variable indicates a factor of *importance* to the subject.
Thus, our sophomore had estimated the need for (lack of) Achievement to be low, and, indeed, she scored high on the variable.

Other questions you may ask about test scores without
revealing personal data in the group are: "Did you score high on
the variables you expected to score high on, and low on the ones
you expected to score low on?" "Are your grades what you would
expect of one who scored as you did on this test?" "How do the
test scores support your educational and vocational choices?"

12. Ask if there are any questions.

Restate basic concepts pointed out during the interpretation,
and have students summarize the discussion.

13. Collect papers that may have been used to illustrate test items, etc., but the Self-Estimate materials are theirs to keep.

You should suggest that they may want to share the test interpretation with their parents, and that you (or someone such as a counselor) will be available for conferences with the parents if they would like to discuss the test data.

14. Invite the students to schedule additional sessions with you or some other teacher or counselor.

You will find that many students will make appointments for additional sessions — not so much to talk about the test data, but as an entree to an individual interview.

Learning to Use These Procedures

After you have had a chance to study the above outline and discussion, read Appendix E, "Case 1: Test Interpretation Using STS-EDS Data." This protocol was taken verbatim from the taped interview of a beginning counselor's use of this procedure for interpreting test data. (Appendix F is the transcript of a GATB interpretation using this self-estimate procedure.)

Next, we would suggest you role-play this procedure with your colleagues. Then you should be able to apply the procedures to individual interpretations and, after a few individual sessions, feel comfortable interpreting tests to small groups.

After you become comfortable with small-group interpretations, we would suggest using the procedures with classroom-size groups. Classroom teachers should be trained to perform this task, and it is usually preferred that the classroom teacher provide the interpretation rather than a counselor or some other outside person. Individual and group interpretations can be equally effective. Figure 69 summarizes some factors to consider in deciding whether to use individual or group interpretation procedures.

Materials Needed for Interpretation

Prior to the test interpretation session, the teacher or counselor should have the following test interpretation materials prepared:

1. Sample test items and/or booklet;
2. Test Interpretation Forms for estimating test scores;
3. Test Interpretation Forms with bands reporting students' scores;
4. Pencils;
5. Diagram of normal distribution on board or paper.

Factors for Consideration	Individual Interpretations	Group Interpretations
M A T E R I A L S	1. Sample test items and/or booklet 2. Test Interpretation Forms for estimating scores 3. Test Interpretation Forms with bands reported 4. Pencils 5. Diagram of normal curve	1. Sample test items and/or booklet 2. Test Interpretation Forms for estimating scores 3. Test Interpretation Forms with bands reported 4. Pencils 5. Diagram of normal curve
T I M E	One hour each, 30 hours total. Additional sessions when required.	1½ hours per group, 10 hours total. Additional sessions when requested.
A D V A N T A G E S	Easy to establish rapport. Individual feels more satisfied with the interpretation. Confidentiality insured. Students have an opportunity to talk about the data.	Saves time. If skillfully handled, members assist in the interpretation. Students may talk over the data with adults and peers.
D I S A D V A N T A G E S	Time consuming. Student may accept interpretation because of authority figure.	Requires skilled leader. Planning group meetings may be difficult. Confidentiality of test data and statements may present difficulty. Students may feel somewhat dissatisfied with the interpretation, or feel forced to explain to the group.

Fig. 69. Factors to Consider in Deciding to Use Individual or Group Test Interpretation Procedures (Time Estimates Based on a 30-Student Group — or One Class)

Example of Interpreter's Role in Test Interpretation

Note: This is an example of the statements which may be made by the interpreter of test scores with an individual high school senior or a group of seniors. The fictional test is the *User's Test of Mental Maturity (Advanced).* The numbers correspond to the numbers on the outline (Figure 64).

1. Establish rapport through appropriate greetings, and begin the test interpretation just as quickly as the student or group is ready.

2. "Recently you took the *User's Test of Mental Maturity (Advanced).* Do you recall what the test was like?" (Show test booklet.)

"This is the test you took about a month ago."

3. "How did you feel about the test when you took it? Was there reason for you to feel that the test was not valid for you? In other words, was there a serious reason or condition present while you were taking the test, such as a severe headache or other illness, misunderstanding of the instructions, and the like, that might have caused you to perform well below your 'average' ability?"

4. "The *User's Test of Mental Maturity (Advanced)* was designed to help you and your teachers estimate your general ability to do school work. This test provides us with a measure of your abilities in three areas: Language — which measures your ability to understand words; Non-Language — which measures your ability to understand non-verbal and numerical materials; and a Total score which combines the Language and Non-Language results to provide the single measure of your general capacity to do school work."

"Before we talk about the results, however, I would like you to recall what the test items were like. Perhaps you would like to look at a few sample questions." (Hand out test booklet to permit brief survey of type of questions.)

"Do you have any questions? Can you describe what the Language part of the test measures? The Non-Language? The Total?"

Often students misunderstand the difference between *ability* and *achievement*; therefore, some effort might be expended at this point in improving their understanding of these concepts. The following questions and answers may serve as a guide to the test interpreter.

"Could a person with average ability make higher grades than a person with high ability? Could a person with low ability make all A's? Sometimes we refer to students as *underachievers* when they perform less well than their measured ability indicates they can perform, and we sometimes refer to those who make better grades than their ability tests indicate they can as *overachievers.* Neither of the words is completely accurate, but they do point up the fact that grades do not always indicate one's ability."

"We mentioned that the *User's Test* provides measures of Language and Non-Language abilities, and a Total or combination of these two measures. What does a score of 25 or 60 or 80 mean to you? In order to make the score meaningful we have to compare your scores with a normative group of students who are similar to yourself. For this comparison, we will use the scores of other students who were enrolled in their second semester of the twelfth grade in this school" (or a representative sampling of schools within the state, region, or nation, as the case may be.) "Therefore, your scores tell how you compare with other seniors in ease or difficulty of learning — since this is what an *ability* test measures."

5. "It might be helpful, now, to look at this diagram to illustrate how we use bands to interpret the results." (Use a diagram of the normal curve, and draw in the band as the explanation is given.)

6. "As you know, most students score about average. This means that there are more scores in the middle of the scale than there are as we move toward the ends of the scale."

7. "In looking at standardized scores we have to consider the standard error of measurement, which means simply that if you took the same test over — or another form of the same test — there would likely be some variation in scores because of chance factors (for example, guessing right on one occasion and wrong on another)."

8. "For this reason we interpret your score as a band rather than a specific point. When we do this we can say with some degree of certainty that your true score would fall somewhere within this band. Of course, we should point out that a test measures only what is asked on the test. In other words, there is much a test does not measure, simply because it is not contained in the questions."

(The interpreter may wish to summarize by asking a few pertinent questions, e.g., "If you retake the same test one week later, would you get the same score? Why? Why not?")

9. Hand out the Test Interpretation Form (Figure 70) to use for self-estimate.

Test Interpretation Form
User's Test of Mental Maturity (Advanced)

Language aptitude — the ability to understand verbal material

Much more difficult	Some- what more difficult	I learn as easily as most	Some- what easier	Much more easily

Non-Language aptitude — the ability to understand non-verbal and numerical material.

Much more difficult	Some- what more difficult	I learn as easily as most	Some- what easier	Much more easily

Total — your general capacity to do school work.

Much more difficult	Some- what more difficult	I learn as easily as most	Some- what easier	Much more easily

Fig. 70. Self-Estimate Form for "User's Test of Mental Maturity (Advanced)"

"This is a self-rating scale which is marked off to correspond to the normal curve. I would like you to estimate your ability to do school work when you compare yourself to other students of your age and grade from a sample representing your school" (region, state, or nation, as the case may be).

"If you feel you learn as easily as most, mark **X** within the average range (anywhere along the line); if less easily, then move to the lower end; or if you learn more easily than the average, then place your mark toward the high end of the scale."

"This will help us to understand how you feel you performed on the test."

"Then, if the results agree — if your estimate is within the reported band — we will know you probably understand what the test measures and your ability in that area. If your test scores and your self-estimate do not agree, then we should try to find out why they are different. However, feel free to agree or disagree, make comments, or ask questions concerning any of the information."

Ask the student or students to read the definitions given on the Test Interpretation Form, ask each student to describe what the definition means to him, and clarify any misconceptions.

10. Hand out the marked Test Interpretation Form. This is the same as the Test Interpretation Form used for self-estimate, except the student's score bands are included.

"Now compare your estimated result with your reported test result. This will be easy if you will mark the X for your estimate from your Test Interpretation Form on the sheet which shows the band in which your score occurred."

"Consider your estimate *accurate* if the estimate falls within the band which is reported."

11. In order to encourage discussion and increase student involvement and understanding, you may wish to raise issues or questions such as these:

"Did you score highest in the area you thought you would? Do your scores agree with your performance in your class work? If not, can you think of any reasons why they did not? Is one score much higher than another? If so, do you feel this is the area in which you perform best? Is remedial work indicated? Do the test scores have any implications for your future plans?"

12. Summarize: Encourage students to make summary statements, raise questions, restate basic concepts, and try to put into their own words what the test data mean to them and how they plan to use the data.

13. Collect papers which are to be left with the professional person responsible for the test data.

14. Encourage students to schedule additional sessions with a teacher or counselor if they feel the need to do so.

I. OTHER ALTERNATIVES

Cumulative Percents

Parents and teachers seem to like percentiles — but not percentile bands — as a method of reporting test scores. Besides the problems inherent in using *numbers*, percentiles offer the additional disadvantages of unequal distances between numbers.

With the use of machines for record keeping, cumulative percent methods have become a popular form for reporting test scores. When cumulative percents are used, small differences in raw scores near the middle of the distribution are magnified, and large differences in raw scores near the extreme of the distribution are minimized. (Figure 71 illustrates this point.)

Raw Score	Frequency	Cumulative Frequency	Percentile Rank (Cumulative Percents)
10	1	72	100
9	2	71	99
8	3	69	96
7	10	66	92
6	20	56	78
5	20	36	50
4	10	16	22
3	3	6	8
2	2	3	4
1	1	1	1

Fig. 71. Raw Scores and Percentile Ranks Obtained by 72 Students

In the above example we can see that 72 students took a test in which the scores ranged from 1 to 10, with most students scoring between 4 and 7. Now, let us illustrate the point made above — *small differences near the middle are magnified, while large differences near the extreme are reduced*. Suppose a student answered the first four items correctly: His percentile rank is 22. Another student answered two more items correctly — six items correct — and his percentile rank is 78. This same relationship holds true for larger, more representative test scores.

Grade Equivalency

Teachers seem to favor grade equivalency as a method of reporting test scores. However, this is probably even less well understood than other forms of score reporting. The grade equivalent is simply another form of presenting the mean (the grade level for the group taking the test) and the deviations from the mean.

Parents and teachers sometimes think the grade equivalent should be interpreted as grade performance, and parents have actually demanded that youngsters be placed in the grade reflected in the score. The higher or lower grade score should be interpreted as a distance from the mean. For example, if a student who is in grade 6.0 takes a test and scores 7.4, this **does not** mean he knows as much about the subject as do students who are in the fourth month of the seventh grade. It **does** mean that the student scored 1.4 grade points above the mean for the normative group. Interpretation for this would be dependent upon the standard deviation for the test. (The discussion of Grade Equivalents in Part I gives additional information concerning the establishment of grade norms and interpretation of grade equivalent scores.)

Graphs and Profiles

Graphs are sometimes used to present test data. We feel that this implies to a student a certain "amount" or "level" in relation to a *total* capacity, i.e., on a scale with a real zero point. The differences between scores, and the highs and lows, are exaggerated in this form of interpretation (see Figure 72). Advertisers have used this technique to exaggerate differences to their advantage for years. Bands around the obtained scores help to overcome part of these problems (see Figure 73).

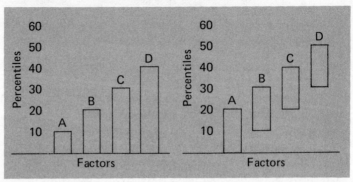

Fig. 72. Graph Showing Performance on a Four-Factor Test

Fig. 73. Graph Showing Same Performance on a Four-Factor Test in Bands

Profiles are even more difficult to comprehend. Highs and lows are often taken literally, and significant differences are not given consideration. Often, sub-test scores may be given the same preciseness as total scores.

The shaded bands in Figure 74 show that scores for Factors B and C are not significantly different, since the bands overlap. If the bands did not overlap — if there were some space between the beginning of one and the ending of the other — this would indicate a significant difference.

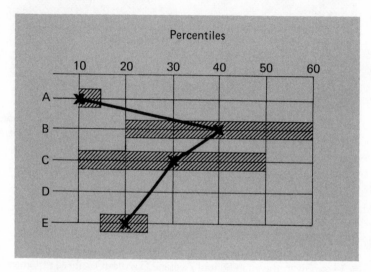

Fig. 74. Profile Used in Reporting Test Data

J. SUGGESTIONS FOR USING GROUP DATA

Although the emphasis in Part II of this manual is on the understanding and interpretation of test results for use with students, the information obtained from the tests should also be used to study the characteristics of the class group, and thus serve administrative and instructional purposes.

The test companies themselves provide free or inexpensive consultative assistance to users, and most companies provide publications in the form of leaflets and booklets to assist in the interpretation of data. However, several suggestions are given below. These are some things we have found helpful in explaining test scores.

Predictions of Grades

Predictions about grades in a particular college may be made from a study of the relationship between the scores on an entrance test — such as the *American College Test* (ACT) or the *Scholastic Aptitude Test* (SAT) published by the College Entrance Examination Board (CEEB) — and grades earned at college. Figure 75 demonstrates this familiar type of predictive validity — in this case, a correlation between high school average and freshman grade average.

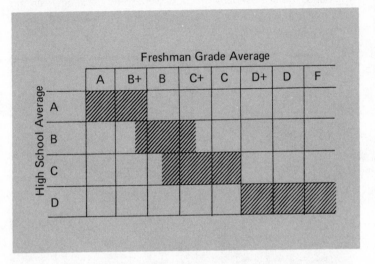

Fig. 75. An Expectancy Table Showing the Chances of Achieving Certain Freshman Grade Averages in One College when Given the High School Average (Two out of three obtained the grades indicated by the bands.)

Scattergrams

A scattergram is a commonly-used technique which helps one to understand group data. The scattergram in Figure 76 shows a comparison of two variables: scores on a verbal ability test and grades in English.

A scattergram can assist the teacher in understanding the achievement of the class in comparison to the scores obtained on a test and also help to identify the student who is not performing at the level of his potential. The scattergram can also help the students and parents understand test data. (If the chart is to be seen by the students and parents it should be constructed with symbols — dots, numbers, or letters — to represent individual students falling in each category.)

The scattergram cannot tell us *why* a student achieves, overachieves, or underachieves the level we would predict for him, but it can help us understand the extent to which this happens.

	Grades in English				
Verbal Ability Scores	F	D	C	B	A
Top 10%	Don	Luther	Dave	Edna Mary	Sue Joe R. Inez Bill T.
Next 15%			Bill K. Wesley Anne Rachel	Joyce Ken Henry	Patsy Ralph
Middle 50%	Frank Emily	Kathy Beth	Carl Tom Joan Janice Jane Cris Jackie Todd	John Gay	Robert Mark Peggy Joe S.
Next 15%		Bob Helen Jack Juan	Harry Dianne	Ray	
Lowest 10%	Fred		Joe N.		

Fig. 76. Ninth-Grade Students Ranked by Grade Average and Verbal Ability Test Scores

Diagram

"Overachieving" and "underachieving" may also be illustrated for the individual or the group by the presentation as shown in Figure 77.

This concept may help us identify students in need of remedial instruction, as well as those who may need more time to master the skills; also, this may prevent us from being complacent about the bright youngster who is doing average work. The use of the words *under-* and *overachievers* is probably misleading, and caution should be exercised in making decisions based on the concept. We sometimes apply it only to the underachievers, forgetting there are other implications.

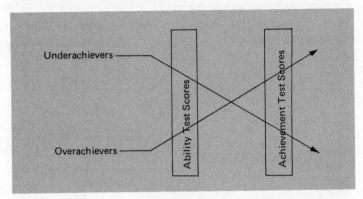

Fig. 77. Relationship of Overachievement and Underachievement

For example, some students who read three, four, or more years below their grade level are doing as well as their ability would indicate they can do. While these students require more time to master the various skills than average students do, they are not in need of *remedial* instruction.

The formula in Figure 78 has been offered as a method of determining expected reading level from IQ-test scores.

$$\text{Expected Reading Grade Level} = GA \times \frac{MA}{CA} + 1$$

Fig. 78. Formula for Determining Expected Reading Grade Level from IQ-Test Scores

In this formula, *GA* represents grade in school and *MA/CA* represents mental age divided by chronological age. As an example, a student who has finished Grade 6 and has an IQ of 135 should be reading at grade level 9.1:

$$(6 \times 1.35) + 1.0 = 8.1 + 1.0 = 9.1$$

This formula is especially helpful in identifying the student who is performing at his actual grade placement level (and may therefore be overlooked), but who needs special help since he is not performing at the level his ability would seem to indicate he could. Such a student will need additional testing in order to identify the specific problem areas where remediation is needed.

K. FINAL EXAM FOR PART II

(This examination is to be completed by the end of Part II. The answers should apply to a real situation — preferably where you are working or will be working next year.)

1. Describe a situation where you will be responsible for a testing program. (This may be as extensive as a regional program or as limited as a specific educational program for a particular school.)

2. State the general and specific objectives of the testing program.

3. What tests (types and, if possible, names) would you use to meet the objectives. (Give a brief description of each.) Be specific.

4. How would you evaluate your testing program?

part 3
ethical
standards
and
issues

A. ASSIGNMENTS

1. Take each test you anticipate administering to others. Score each, and write an explanation and interpretation of the test data.

2. Take the range of ages for all of the students you teach or for whom you are responsible for program or evaluation, and observe one child of each age for one full hour. Keep a verbatim description of all of his/her behavior for that hour. For example, if you are a counselor for Grades 1–8, the students probably range in age from 5-year-olds to 15-year-olds. Thus, you will choose one 5-year-old, one 6-year-old, one 7-year-old, etc., and observe that child (without his knowledge) for one full hour. (The purpose of this activity is to provide data for understanding youngsters, as well as practicing a procedure for understanding a child through planned observation.)

3. Using the Critical Situations in Section F of Part III as a basis for a group study of ethics, have each group member write his reactions to each situation, and then discuss these situations and responses in relation to the APGA code of ethics on testing.

B. THE IMPACT OF TESTING

About a quarter of a billion dollars is spent on tests every year, with an estimated time expenditure of fifty million hours of testing. What a waste of time, money, and energy if the data are not used! What a waste if the data are used as a polite explanation for labeling, or as a sophisticated procedure for stratifying society, i.e., developing an "aristocracy of the intellect."

Stratification according to accident of birth is somehow unpalatable to a society based upon the democratic precepts of equality, but the "accident of intellect," while blamed on inheritance and the denied responsibility of the environment, is — or at least has been — acceptable. Recently we have seen a healthy resistance to the idea that we can measure the intellect objectively, without the contaminating factor of cultural bias. More and more it behooves the educator, the counselor, and the examiner to look at the testing instrument as a tool to be used with *extreme caution* and care, to be cognizant of the limitations in its use *and* of the dynamics involved in the interpretation and application of data in decision-making.

Information about a student and *understanding* a student are two different things. We can assimilate vast amounts of data about something or someone and still have little or no understanding of it or him. We are much less concerned about your skills as a test technician than we are about your skills as an educator who uses test and non-test data effectively and accurately. One over-riding attitude we hope to foster is the use of tests to identify potential, rather than their use to measure limitations. We feel this would minimize a great deal of the harmful effects of testing.

We also need to consider carefully the impact of testing on our school curriculum. When we judge performance of an individual or a school on the basis of tests standardized on national norms, we implicitly set as the goals of our educational program those set by the author of the test; and we generally explicitly set the mean for the published norms as the acceptable standard of achievement.

The unanswered and often-debated question, especially in recent years, is just how much common agreement we do have concerning our educational goals. In a like manner, we also question the degree that all children are alike on those factors, known and unknown, that influence test performance. An example: A bilingual child was tested using only one language — English. The child's test score indicated retardation. Yet, when the same child was tested using both languages, the test yielded a score well above average. How much harm is done to a child when the wrong instrument is used to evaluate ability and/or performance?

Thus, it is not enough to evaluate only the instrument: We must also evaluate the limitations of an instrument (and allow for these), and the use to be made of the data. Data that are appropriately gathered, appropriately used, and accurately applied can increase the probability of good decisions being made by and for an individual; otherwise, to test is a useless exercise.

C. RESPONSIBILITY FOR TEST USE

Who is responsible for the appropriate and accurate use of tests and test data, the publisher, the author, or the test user? While all professional people are expected to exercise good judgment and restraint, nevertheless the primary responsibility for using the instruments must fall to the test user.

Someone has commented that any test will find a good market if it meets the following three criteria: 1. Its name or scores imply a simple construct when measuring a complex construct, such as intelligence; 2. It is packaged for easy administration and scoring; and 3. It can be administered during a regular class period. One hopes the test user is more sophisticated than this comment suggests, yet we know that inadequate and inappropriate instruments are used every day. They are used to make decisions *about* students, groups, personnel, etc., and occasionally are interpreted to the individual for his use in making decisions about himself.

Sometimes the test user seems to suspect that the instruments he is using are not valid. When confronted with a request for interpretation of a score derived from such instruments, he will say something to the effect that, "Well, it's just a score," or "It really doesn't tell us much." Yet, these same scores will be used to make decisions about a person — e.g., to label, place in special groups and, sometimes, even to grade students on performance. (We have heard of teachers recording scores obtained on *ability* tests in their class record and grade book!) If questioned at this point about why the scores were used as a basis for the decision if they "really don't tell us much," the user will comment, "But it's the best we have!" Such circular arguments are advanced to avoid the issue. There are many valid tests to measure the outcomes of most well-specified and clearly-defined objectives, and using inadequate (i.e., invalid, unreliable) instruments is totally unwarranted.

A test user must study a test and its accompanying technical materials in order to make logical and "good" choices of an instrument. Of the thousands of tests published every year, many do not offer even the minimum technical data for evaluating them in terms of reliability and validity. In some situations where the information about the tests is adequate, the purchaser does not determine the effectiveness of the instrument for meeting his purposes. We have had test users tell us they have used tests and test results without ever having read the test items or analyzed the validity of the test for their purposes. Some individuals and some agencies rely upon an individual outside the agency, such as a psychological consultant, to choose the tests to be administered and to interpret the test data — without even knowing the rationale for the items used in the test. Thus, test use has come under criticism — and rightly so, when inappropriate and inadequate tests are used, and when invalid decisions are made on the basis of test data.

D. ETHICS AND THE LAW

While professional organizations have spent a great deal of energy and time establishing guidelines to protect themselves and their clients, a movement has been underway to move many of the judgments out of the realm of professional consideration and into the jurisdiction of the courts. Ross, DeYoung, and Cohen, the authors of the article "Confrontation: Special Education Placement and the Law,"[1] warn us that, "Educators will not be able to continue to hide behind the indefensible and inexcusable use of intelligence test scores as the primary basis for identifying, labeling and placing children in special classes." They go on to make a very convincing argument against psychologists' and educators' explanations and arguments for the misuse and misinterpretation of test data. Their points are so crucial to our needs, their position is so well stated, and the application of their logic extends so far beyond the profession of special education to which they are primarily addressing their remarks, that the article is reproduced in its entirety as Appendix G.

E. EVERYONE IS ACCOUNTABLE

As we have seen, collectively and individually, and ethically as well as legally, we individually must assume responsibility for our own use of tests. While test distributors attempt to follow the guidelines set down in *Ethical Standards of Psychologists* (adopted by the American Psychological Association in 1952) concerning the distribution of tests, it is not expected that the test publishers can or should perform extensive investigations of potential users. Instead, it is essential that every test user evaluate his own competencies and qualifications for using tests, and perhaps discuss these qualifications with recognized experts in the field. Also, you should carefully study the code of ethics of your professional organization or organizations when there are questions relevant to the use of test data and other information. The Ethical Standards of the American Personnel and Guidance Association provide the following guidelines concerning testing:

APGA Ethical Standards[2]
Section C
Testing

1. The primary purpose of psychological testing is to provide objective and comparative measures for use in self-evaluation or evaluation by others of general or specific attributes.

---

[1] Ross, S. R., Jr., DeYoung, H. G., and Cohen, J. S. *Exceptional Children.* 1971, 38 (1), 5-12.

[2] Reprinted with permission of the American Personnel and Guidance Association, Washington, D. C.

2. Generally, test results constitute only one of a variety of pertinent data for personnel and guidance decisions. It is the member's responsibility to provide adequate orientation or information to the examinee(s) so that the results of testing may be placed in proper perspective with other relevant factors.

3. When making any statements to the public about tests and testing care must be taken to give accurate information and to avoid any false claims or misconceptions.

4. Different tests demand different levels of competence for administration, scoring, and interpretation. It is, therefore, the responsibility of the member to recognize the limits of his competence and to perform only those functions which fall within his preparation and competence.

5. In selecting tests for use in a given situation or with a particular client the member must consider not only general but also specific validity, reliability, and appropriateness of the test(s).

6. Tests should be administered under the same conditions which were established in their standardization. Except for research purposes explicitly stated, any departures from these conditions, as well as unusual behavior or irregularities during the testing session which may affect the interpretation of the test results, must be fully noted and reported. In this connection, unsupervised test-taking or the use of tests through the mails are of questionable value.

7. The value of psychological tests depends in part on the novelty to persons taking them. Any prior information, coaching, or reproduction of test materials tends to invalidate test results. Therefore, test security is one of the professional obligations of the member.

8. The member has the responsibility to inform the examinee(s) as to the purpose of testing. The criteria of examinee's welfare and/or explicit prior understanding with him should determine who the recipients of the test results may be.

9. The member should guard against the appropriation, reproduction, or modification of published tests or parts thereof without expressed permission and adequate recognition of the original author or publisher.

Regarding the preparation, publication, and distribution of tests, reference should be made to:

"Tests and Diagnostic Techniques" - - Report of the Joint Committee of the American Psychological Association, American

Educational Research Association, and National Council of Measurements used in Education, Supplement to *Psychological Bulletin,* 1954, *2,* 1 - 38.

F. INTERPRETING CRITICAL TEST SITUATIONS

Consider each critical situation given below, and determine the professional responsibility you have in each situation. You may find it helpful to discuss these situations with your colleagues, and these problems might also be used effectively for in-service workshops or conferences on the use of test data. In each situation, decide *what you should do.*

Critical Situation 1:

In the high school where you are a new teacher, the principal sends a register with the standardized test scores for all students to all teachers. The raw scores and grade equivalents are reported. No other data are provided. When you go into the teacher's lounge at your break, you are confronted with a discussion of the test data. Most of the teachers have relatives in the school, and much of the "interpretation" is to point out "how smart" certain relatives are. Also, you are surprised that the grade equivalent scores are misunderstood. *What should you do?*

Critical Situation 2:

A program has been approved for your school which calls for testing the students with the *Wechsler Intelligence Scale for Children* (WISC). A counselor, who has had no special training in the use of individual tests, offers to administer the tests after school hours and on Saturdays for a very reasonable fee. You raise the question about his competencies in this area, and he states that he has seen the WISC given, that he has read and studied the research, and that he plans to study the manual before giving the first test. The program coordinator is satisfied with the explanation, since the counselor has had a course in testing and has been helpful in explaining the test scores for the school testing program. *What should you do?*

Critical Situation 3:

You are the coordinator of the testing program for your school. A teacher brings her test data to you and exclaims, "I have finished with these test grades. The grades are what I expected, but I *do like* to have them in my class record book when I make out report cards. It helps me show parents why their children make such bad grades sometimes. I surely am glad we have the IQ scores for my classes." *What should you do?*

Critical Situation 4:

Children entering Tate Junior High School are given a standardized test of ability and an achievement test in reading and math before completing the seventh grade at the feeder school. The test data are sent to Tate in May, and at that time the principal and teachers at Tate assign the students to one of three tracks: advanced, regular, and general. The assignments are made on the basis of the reading test scores only, with the explanation; "A student has to be able to read to do anything in school."

You are employed as a counselor in one of the feeder schools. You have been informed of the placements of the students, with the notation: "You can have a chance to tell the parents and students to make it easier for them to adjust to the new school next fall." *What should you do?*

Critical Situation 5:

You are a new principal in the school. The counselor who was there last year gave lots of tests and filed the scores, which he marked "confidential," in the counselor's office. (He apparently intended the files for counselor use only, since the tests he gave were not a part of the regularly-scheduled tests administered to all students.) A parent has come in and demanded to see the file on his child. *What should you do?*

Critical Situation 6:

The local newspaper hopes to do an article on the "new math" program, and has asked to be allowed to have group test data for the past two years for comparison purposes. You are the principal. *What should you do?*

Critical Situation 7:

A counselor in your school has been using the test scores obtained from a college entrance examination to identify youngsters for "counseling." From the feedback you get from the students, as well as statements made by the counselor, you are fairly certain that the counselor is using the test scores to convince students that they "should" or "should not" go to college. The students receive only a raw score interpretation of their performance on the college entrance examination. You feel the data are not valid for the purposes for which they are being used. *What should you do?*

Critical Situation 8:

Sam, a student in your homeroom, asks to be allowed to take French I. His father's firm is transferring him to France next year, and the family will move there with him. Sam tells you that the assistant principal will not allow him to enroll in a foreign language class, since he scored below the cutoff score on the English Achievement Test which is used for placing students in French. Sam is an average student in most of his work. You explain the situation to the assistant principal and ask that Sam be allowed to take French. The assistant principal refuses, with the explanation: "A rule's a rule." *What should you do?*

Critical Situation 9:

A new test is being added to the school's testing program to measure students' awareness of current events and solving everyday problems. The new teachers in the social studies department suspect that the test is being added to measure their effectiveness, since the principal has stated on several occasions that he feels that department should teach "about practical things for our world today." Several of the teachers have decided to implement a series of "games" to teach students to think through everyday problems and have added a "current events quiz" for Friday's class. You are on the social studies curriculum study committee. *What should you do?*

Critical Situation 10:

A teacher in your school is also a graduate student in education. As a part of his academic program, he is studying the personality characteristics and family backgrounds of slow learners. He has asked permission to come to your class to give two personality tests and complete a questionnaire on each child. You ask him if he has the permission of the parents to give the tests. He says, "No, but the principal says it's OK, and I need it for a class research project." *What should you do?*

Critical Situation 11:

You are responsible for working with students identified as underprivileged. A special federally funded program offered in your community is designed to train low-income students as paraprofessionals. The program offers participants subsistence, travel, and allowances for dependents. Your students have expressed interest in the program and have taken the qualifying examinations.

You are surprised that many bright students are turned down for the program on the basis of the test scores, and that to fill the quota for the courses, average-income students are allowed to enter the program. Upon inquiry about the test, you learn many items appear to be culturally biased. Questions which appear to you to have little face validity are contained on the test. Items such as: "(A) How many holes are on a golf course?" and "(B) Which is the 'best buy' on linens?" are outside the experience of the students with whom you work. Thus, you question the fairness of the test. *What should you do?*

Critical Situation 12:

The parents of one of your students are greatly distressed. They have a younger child at home who they suspect is "not quite right." In a magazine they had seen an advertisement for a test which they could administer at home to help them evaluate the performance level of their child. They ordered the test, administered it, and scored it. Their interpretation of the score upset them, and they came to you with a plea for help with the child. *What should you do?*

G. RECAPITULATION

Test data might be considered as snapshots of a person's performance at a given time, and as the analogy implies, the picture may be very misleading (and certainly can be made misleading). At the same time, a picture has the *potential* of providing a "study in still life" which can be far more accurate than mere words.

As human beings we apparently have a need to simplify. For example, we see the political extremes — right and left — with their simplistic answers to complex questions drawing national attention and winning applause from a large segment of society. *People want simple answers to complex questions.* The more complex the problem, the more gullible we are about its oversimplification — the more diligently we struggle for *the* answer.

This attitude is probably one explanation of why we look to such inventions as the computer to provide *the* answer. One couple explained their choice of colors and decor for their home as "computer decorated." What data went into the computer for the decision? Who decided what factors were related, and in what ways? These questions were not even considered, and whether the couple liked the house was beside the point, since the decision was "accurate." In a similar fashion, we look to tests to provide the answers to our educational or employment problems. In the use of our test data, we tend to substitute a simple *number* or a simple name for a complex construct.

Teachers and counselors sometimes have a blind faith in numbers such as test scores because the tests are scored by a computer, which makes the numbers *official* — if not sacred. One psychologist tells of giving an individual intelligence test to a student who was referred by the school for that purpose. After the examination the psychologist noted that the group intelligence test score which had been recorded on the child's school record was not even reasonably accurate and suggested to the teacher that she should correct the permanent record. However, the teacher informed the psychologist that the permanent record data could not be changed and were indeed accurate, "since the test was scored by the computer." No amount of explanation convinced her that the score was in error.

Simply to "send tests off" to be scored influences some teachers and parents to believe that the data are accurate. There seems to be a direct correlation between the degree to which the tests are removed from local control (construction, selection, and scoring) and the assumed validity and authenticity of the evaluation — at least in some sections of the country. This is probably tied to the belief in the infallibility of the *expert,* or in the conclusions drawn from *the study* that was made.

Tests should be carefully chosen to measure what one wishes to measure, applied with caution to obtain data for specific reasons, and appropriately evaluated for any limiting factors such as language barriers or cultural biases. The test data that are obtained should be put to use for and, in most instances, interpreted to the person who takes the test. In all situations, one should take cognizance of the ethical considerations for the use of tests.

Appendix A
Answers to Study Questions
Part I

SQ 1:   tall, short
Democrat, Republican
pro, con, indifferent
zip code numbers
social security numbers

SQ 2:   yes

SQ 3:   batting averages
standing in graduating class
place in a contest or race (He finished first, second, etc.)
order as demonstrated in a spelling bee

SQ 4:   yes

SQ 5:   temperature as measured on the Centigrade (Celsius) scale
and on the Fahrenheit scale
scores on some well-constructed and nationally-normed
standardized tests can be considered interval scores

SQ 6:   yes

SQ 7:   monetary system
height
weight
volume

SQ 8:   Yes, if we used a temperature scale which has an absolute
zero, such as the Kelvin Scale.

SQ 9:   one

SQ 10:

Test Score	f
5	/
4	//
3	///
2	//
1	/

SQ 11: a. test scores
b. frequencies
c. 2/3 to 3/4 the length of the horizontal axis
d. a graph illustrating the number of times each
score occurs

SQ 12:

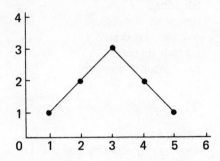

SQ 13: a. 45
b. $i = 3$
c. apparent: 4; real: 3.5, 4.5
d. apparent: 2, 4; real: 1.5, 4.5
e. 3

SQ 14:

Score	f	cf
5	1	9
4	2	8
3	3	6
2	2	3
1	1	1

SQ 15:
9/9 X 100 = 100
8/9 X 100 = 89
6/9 X 100 = 67
3/9 X 100 = 33
1/9 X 100 = 11

SQ 16: Percentile rank tells the percent of people or scores which
fall below the upper real limit of the interval of that score.

SQ 17: 3

SQ 18: most: The mode is the number which occurs most frequently in a group of scores, or the raw score which is
obtained by the largest number of students.

SQ 19:

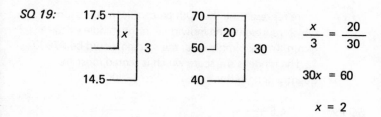

$$\frac{x}{3} = \frac{20}{30}$$

$$30x = 60$$

$$x = 2$$

17.5 − 2 = 15.5. The median or fiftieth percentile is equal to a raw score of 15.5.

SQ 20:

67 ⌐
       17
50 ⌐   34
33 ———

3.5 ⌐
        x
           1
2.5 ———

$$\frac{x}{1} = \frac{17}{34}$$

$$34x = 17$$

$$x = .5$$

3.5 − .5 = 3.0. The median is equal to a raw score of 3.0.

SQ 21: The median is the point above and below which 50% of the scores fall.

SQ 22: Add the numbers (the sum of)

SQ 23: $\Sigma X = 12$

SQ 24: $M = \dfrac{5 + 2 + 3 + 1 + 4 + 2 + 3 + 3 + 4}{9} = 3$

SQ 25: $M = 3$

SQ 26: median = 2.5

SQ 27: No. The median would be a more accurate measure of central tendency since the mean is very sensitive to extreme scores.

SQ 28: Since this distribution is badly skewed, the one large salary "pulled" the mean in that direction. The mean, therefore, does not accurately indicate the middle section, and it is misleading to report it as the measure of central tendency.

A more accurate description of the center would be given by the median and the mode. The median is the

113

score representing the 50th percentile, or the score which represents the individual in the middle of the group. In this simple case, the median would be $7000.

The mode is the score which is scored most frequently and, in this case, it is also $7000.

SQ 29:

4.5 ⌐————⌐
     | x | 1
3.5 ⌐————⌐

89 ⌐————⌐
   | 14 | 22
75 ⌐————⌐
67 ————

$$\frac{x}{1} = \frac{14}{22}$$

$$x = .64$$

a. $4.5 - .64 = 3.86 = Q_3$

2.5 ⌐————⌐
     | x | 1
1.5 ⌐————⌐

33 ⌐————⌐
   | 8 | 22
25 ⌐————⌐
11 ————

$$\frac{x}{1} = \frac{8}{22}$$

$$x = .36$$

b. $2.5 - .36 = 2.14 = Q_1$

c. $\dfrac{3.86 - 2.14}{2} = \dfrac{1.72}{2} = .86 = Q$

d. The semi-interquartile range is used when your data are ordinally scaled, or when you have used the median as your measure of central tendency.

SQ 30: x is the deviation score $X - M$, which is the result of subtracting the mean from the score, while X is the raw score.

SQ 31: a. when we assume the data are distributed intervally, or when we have used the mean as our measure of central tendency.

b. $S = \sqrt{\dfrac{\Sigma x^2}{N}}$

1. Calculate mean
2. Obtain deviations by subtracting the mean from each score
3. Square the deviation scores
4. Add the squared deviations
5. Divide by N
6. Find the square root

SQ 32:

	x	x^2
5 - 3	= 2	4
4 - 3	= 1	1
4 - 3	= 1	1
3 - 3	= 0	0
3 - 3	= 0	0
3 - 3	= 0	0
2 - 3	= -1	1
2 - 3	= -1	1
1 - 3	= -2	4
$M = 3$		$\Sigma x^2 = 12$

$$S = \sqrt{\frac{\Sigma x^2}{N}}$$

$$= \sqrt{\frac{12}{9}}$$

$$= \sqrt{1.33}$$

$$S = 1.15$$

SQ 33: With raw data when the mean is not a whole number, when we have a large N, or when a calculator is available. Data rarely yield a mean that is a whole number, which makes the deviation method arithmetically cumbersome. With a desk calculator and a little practice, you will find it much easier to use the raw score method.

SQ 34: X^2 is the raw score squared.

SQ 35: 1.15 is the *S* using the raw score method.

X ($N = 9$)	X^2
5	25
4	16
4	16
3	9
3	9
3	9
2	4
2	4
1	1
$M = 3$	$\Sigma X^2 = 93$

$$S = \sqrt{\frac{\Sigma X^2}{N} - M^2}$$

$$= \sqrt{\frac{93}{9} - 9}$$

$$= \sqrt{10.33 - 9}$$

$$= \sqrt{1.33}$$

$$S = 1.15$$

SQ 36: 0, 1

SQ 37: positive, negative

SQ 38: $z = \dfrac{X - M}{S}$; RS 6: $z = \dfrac{6 - 4}{2} = +1.0$;

RS 5: $z = \dfrac{5 - 4}{2} = +0.5$; RS 4: $z = \dfrac{4 - 4}{2} = 0$;

RS 3: $z = \dfrac{3 - 4}{2} = -0.5$; RS 2; $z = \dfrac{2 - 4}{2} = -1.0$;

RS 1: $z = \dfrac{1 - 4}{2} = -1.5$.

SQ 39: a. 68.26
b. 15.73
c. 34.13

SQ 40: Percentiles are ordinal data, *z* scores are interval data.

SQ 41: so it is not necessary to have negative numbers or decimals.

SQ 42:

$$z\ (+1.5)\quad T = 50 + 1.5(10)$$

$$= 50 + 15$$

$$= 65$$

$$z\ (+1.0)\quad T = 50 + 1(10)$$

$$= 50 + 10$$

$$= 60$$

$$z\ (+0.5)\quad T = 50 + .5(10)$$

$$= 50 + 5$$

$$= 55$$

$$z\ (0)\quad T = 50 + 0(10)$$

$$= 50$$

$$z\ (-0.5)\quad T = 50 + (-.5)(10)$$

$$= 50 + (-5)$$

$$= 45$$

$$z\ (-1.0)\quad T = 50 + (-1.0)(10)$$

$$= 50 + (-10)$$

$$= 40$$

$$z(-1.5) \quad T = 50 + (-1.5)(10)$$

$$= 50 + (-15)$$

$$= 35$$

SQ 43: A correlation coefficient is an index or number which indicates the relationship between two sets of scores or data.

SQ 44: a score for each individual on two measures

SQ 45: +1.00 or −1.00

SQ 46: As the scores on one measure increase, the scores on the other measure decrease.

SQ 47: no relationship at all

SQ 48:
0
1.0
−0.75
0
−0.75
1.5
1.5

SQ 49: 2.50

SQ 50: $N = 7$

SQ 51: $r = .357$ or $.36$

SQ 52: It is necessary to convert all scores to z scores first, and this becomes cumbersome if there is a large number of raw scores.

SQ 53:
a. ΣX = add up all raw scores on Test 1.
b. ΣXY = multiply each score on Test 1 by its counterpart on Test 2. Then add all the products.
c. ΣY^2 = square all scores on Test 2, and add them.

SQ 54: Usually the scores would vary — sometimes they would be higher and sometimes lower.

SQ 55: Test-retest reliability — the correlation of scores when an individual has taken the same test twice, or it has been administered to the same people on two different occasions.

SQ 56: Comparable-forms reliability — the correlation of scores from two tests which supposedly measure the same behaviors, and which are given at the same time.

SQ 57: Split-half reliability — the correlation of the score on the odd-numbered items with the score on the even-numbered items of a single test.

SQ 58: The split-half reliability technique overcomes the problem of giving the same test at different times, or of writing two forms of the same test which are truly comparable.

SQ 59: $r_{xx} = \dfrac{2(.80)}{1 + .80} = \dfrac{1.60}{1.80} = .89$

SQ 60: The standard error of measurement tells us the distance from the obtained score, or the bounds, within which the individual's true score could fall.

SQ 61: $S_M = S \sqrt{1 - .84} = 3 \sqrt{.16} = 3(.4) = 1.2$

SQ 62: If John were to take the test again, 68% of the time he would score between 48 and 52; 96% of the time he would score between 46 and 54; and 4% of the time he would score higher than 54 or lower than 46.

SQ 63: *Validity* indicates how well a test measures what it is supposed to measure.

SQ 64: *Concurrent validity* compares a test to a criterion measure obtained at the same time.

SQ 65: *Predictive validity* compares a test to a future event or criterion measure.

SQ 66: **Content validity** identifies how well the test samples the type of behavior which it is designed to measure.

SQ 67: **Construct validity** deals with the underlying theory of the test.

Appendix B

Glossary of Statistical Terms

Band — An area which includes the obtained score of an individual and the standard error of measurement. If we use one standard error of measurement on either side of the obtained score, we are 68% certain that we have included the score the individual would obtain on a retest. If we use two standard errors of measurement on either side of the obtained score, we are 95% certain.

Central Tendency — Measures of the central positions for a group. In statistics this average may be expressed as a mean, median, or mode.

Deviation — The distance of a raw score from the mean. The formula is:

$$x = (X - M)$$

where x = the deviation;
               X = the raw score; and
               M = the mean.

Mean — The arithmetic average. It is computed by dividing the sum of scores by the total number of scores. The formula is:

$$M = \frac{\Sigma X}{N}$$

where M = the mean;
               Σ = the sum of;
               X = the raw score; and
               N = the number.

Median — The point on a distribution which has equal numbers of cases above and below it.

Mode — The one value in a distribution which occurs most frequently.

Normal Curve — An infinite number of separate values or cases that graphically form a symmetrical bell-shaped distribution with the mean, median, and mode having the same value, and equal numbers of cases on either side of the central axis.

Norms — The statistics that describe the results obtained by a specified group on a specified test.

Population — All of the people, things, cases, or data about which an inference is made.

Range — The difference between the highest and lowest scores on a test. The formula is:

$$Range = HX - LX$$

where HX = the high score; and
LX = the low score.

(*Note:* Some authors add one to the highest score — to *include* both the top and bottom score.)

Raw Score — The direct result of the test, i.e., the number of correct answers that a person obtains from a test.

Reliability — The accuracy or consistency with which a test measures what it actually does measure.

Reliability Coefficient — The degree of correspondence or relative standing between scores obtained on two measures by the same group. The formula is:

$$r = \frac{\Sigma z_1 z_2}{N}$$

where r = the reliability coefficient;
Σ = the sum of;
z_1 = the z score for the first measure;
z_2 = the z score for the second measure; and
N = the number of students.

Example of Computation:

	z Score Test 1		z Score Test 2	
Sam	z	X	z	= Product
Joan	z	X	z	= Product
Etc.		Etc.		Σ Products
				No. of Students

Sample — A portion of some *population* about which an inference is made.

Standard Deviation — The square root of the average of the squared deviations from the means. The formulas are:

$$S = \sqrt{\frac{\Sigma x^2}{N}}$$

or

$$SD = S = \sqrt{\frac{\Sigma (X - M)^2}{N}}$$

where
S or SD = the standard deviation;
Σx^2 = the sum of the deviations squared;
N = the number;
$X - M$ = the deviation from the mean; and
$\Sigma (X - M)^2$ = the sum of the deviations squared.

The steps involved are:
1. Compute the mean, M.
2. Subtract the mean from each score, $X - M$.
3. Square the deviations, $(X - M)^2$.
4. Sum the squared deviations.
5. Divide the summed deviations from the mean by the number.
6. Take the square root of the number.

Standard Error of Measurement (S_M) — An estimate of the deviation of a set of obtained scores from their "true" scores. The S_M is dependent upon the standard deviation of the distribution of obtained scores and upon the coefficient of reliability (r) of the test from which the distribution of scores was obtained. The formula for determining the standard error of measurement is:

$$S_M = S_X \sqrt{1 - r_{XX}}$$

where
S_M = the standard error of measurement;
S_X = the standard deviation of the scores; and
r_{XX} = the reliability of the test.

(Note: Figure 62 in Part II provides a table for estimating the standard error of measurement.)

Standard Score — A measure of relative standing that has a constant relationship to raw scores and is expressed in standard deviation units. The formula for a standard *z* score is:

$$z = \frac{X - M}{S}$$

where

z = the standard score;
$X - M$ = the deviation of the raw score from the mean; and
SD or S = the standard deviation.

Standardized Test — A measuring instrument which must be administered under prescribed conditions and scored in a predetermined manner. The interpretation of the results is in terms of the performances of a normative group drawn from a representative *sample* for a prescribed *population* of a specific age or educational level.

"True Score" — A score that is free from *chance* factors and errors of measurement; it represents an individual's true level of performance on a test.

Validity — The extent to which a test measures what it purports to measure.

Variance — An index of how much the individuals in a group deviate from the average for the group. The formula is:

$$S^2 = \frac{\Sigma x^2}{N}$$

where

S^2 = the variance;
Σx^2 = the sum of the deviations squared (Σ = the sum of $x^2 = [X - M]^2$); and
N = the number.

Appendix C

Test: MUST Parts I and II

A. Multiple Choice:

Directions: Put the letter for the best answer on the line provided for each question.

_____ 1. If a mathematics test and an art test correlated −.95, students who scored high in mathematics would

   a. always score high in art.

   b. always have lowest scores in art.

   c. tend to score low in art.

   d. tend to score very high in art.

_____ 2. An achievement test is used to

   a. predict what all students will do in the future.

   b. sample behaviors that indicate performance in a given situation.

   c. measure personality traits.

   d. determine interests and attitudes.

_____ 3. When comparing students' test scores with standardized test norms, the norms should be compiled from

   a. a large, representative population.

   b. standards set by individual teachers.

   c. the students' average test scores in all classes.

   d. records of performance of past classes.

_____ 4. The correlation between a reading-comprehension test and a history test is .85. If a student scored above the mean in reading comprehension, he is _____ to be above the mean on the history test.

   a. likely

   b. certain

   c. unlikely

   d. cannot tell

_____ 5. Which of the following correlations has the *least* predictive power?

   a. −1.00

   b. −.23

   c. .17

   d. .50

6. If a person's raw score is 80 on a test having a mean of 65 and a standard deviation of 10, his z score is
   a. -1.5.
   b. 1.5.
   c. 2.5.
   d. 15.0.

7. About what percent of the cases in a normal distribution will fall between one standard deviation below the mean and one standard deviation above the mean?
   a. 14%
   b. 34%
   c. 68%
   d. 95%

8. A large value of the standard deviation for a set of test scores means that the scores are
   a. all high.
   b. all low.
   c. closely clustered about the mean.
   d. widely dispersed.

9. If the scores in a distribution are very closely clustered about the mean, then the distribution has a
   a. large variance.
   b. small variance.
   c. large mean.
   d. small mean.

10. The mean of a set of test scores is the
   a. average squared.
   b. middle score.
   c. score occurring most frequently.
   d. sum of the scores divided by the number of scores.

11. If a test is given to a group of high school students to determine how well they will do in college, the function of the test is
   a. assessment.
   b. prediction.
   c. trait measurement.
   d. evaluation.

12. For a perfectly normal distribution, the mean is

    a. equal to the median and the mode.

    b. between the median and the mode.

    c. greater than the median, but less than the mode.

    d. greater than the mode, but less than the median.

13. If a person receives a score of 60 on a test with a standard error of measurement of 5, there is about a 95% chance that his true score lies within the confidence interval of

    a. 55 - 65.

    b. 60 - 65.

    c. 45 - 75.

    d. 50 - 70.

14. Reliability is an index of

    a. how well a test measures what it proposes to measure.

    b. the relationship between a measure and its criterion.

    c. variability of performance on a test.

    d. the stability or consistency of measurement.

15. What is the standard error of measurement for a test with a standard deviation of 5 and a reliability coefficient of .84?

    a. 0.164

    b. 1.0

    c. 2.0

    d. 4.2

16. What percent of a sample lies between z scores of 0 and −2?

    a. 48%

    b. 95%

    c. 50%

    d. 16%

17. The best measure of the variability of a test is the

    a. semi-interquartile range.

    b. range of raw scores.

    c. standard deviation.

    d. average deviation.

_____ 18. John obtained a raw score of 10 on a test. The standard error of measurement for this test is 2.00. Which of the following would be true?

    a. Two-thirds of the time his score would be between 8 and 12 on the next administration of the test.

    b. Providing he didn't cheat, his score would be 10 on the next administration of the test.

    c. Two-thirds of the time his score would be between 10 and 12 on the next administration of the test.

    d. His score would be a function of the distribution of the class, and no more definite statement can be made about it.

_____ 19. A teacher computed a correlation of .92 between scores on a reading test and scores on a current affairs test. He was justified in concluding that, as measured by these two tests,

    a. knowledge of current affairs and reading ability are closely related.

    b. knowledge of current affairs and reading ability are unrelated.

    c. knowledge of current affairs and reading ability are perfectly related.

    d. knowledge of current affairs is highly related to good reading ability.

_____ 20. Which of the following correlations provides the *best* basis for prediction?

    a. −.90

    b. .00

    c. .30

    d. .80

_____ 21. In determining validity, it would be best to correlate scores on a test with

    a. other scores on the same test.

    b. some independent measure of a criterion.

    c. some comparable form of the test.

    d. all of these.

B. Matching:

Directions: For each question, write the letter from the right column that matches the statement in the left column.

____ 22. mean

____ 23. the extent to which two tests are related

____ 24. a method of measuring reliability of a test

____ 25. variance

____ 26. the statistics which describe the performance of a specific group on some test

____ 27. standard error of measurement

____ 28. the extent to which a test is consistent in measuring what it measures

____ 29. the extent to which a test measures what it attempts to measure

____ 30. the middle score in a set of ranked scores

____ 31. a crude measure of the spread of scores

____ 32. standard deviation

____ 33. the direct result of a test

____ 34. the deviation of a score from the mean expressed as a standard z score

____ 35. a scale in which the distances between each number and the next are equal

____ 36. a correlation coefficient which indicates perfect relationship between two tests

____ 37. a correlation coefficient which indicates no relationship between two tests

a. $r = 1.00$

b. $\dfrac{\Sigma X}{N}$

c. $\dfrac{\Sigma x^2}{N}$

d. $S \sqrt{1 - r}$

e. validity

f. reliability

g. norms

h. split half

i. correlation coefficient

j. $X - M$

k. $(S - M)$

l. median

m. predictive function

n. $\sqrt{\dfrac{\Sigma x^2}{N}}$

o. range

p. raw score

q. $\dfrac{X - M}{S}$

r. interval scale

s. ordinal scale

t. $r = 0.00$

u. $r = 0.50$

C. Statistics:

Directions: For questions 38-45, write the formulas requested, then compute the statistics for these test scores.

> An achievement test was administered to a high school class and the following raw scores were obtained: 2, 3, 4, 5, 6, 7, 8.

What is the *mean* of these scores?

      38. Formula: $M =$ _____

      39. Answer: _____

What are the *deviation scores* for these seven people?

      40. Formula: $x =$ _____

      41. Answer: a. $2 =$ _____

                 b. $3 =$ _____

                 c. $4 =$ _____

                 d. $5 =$ _____

                 e. $6 =$ _____

                 f. $7 =$ _____

                 g. $8 =$ _____

What is the *standard deviation* of this test?

      42. Formula: $S =$ _____

      43. Answer: _____

What are the *standard z scores* for these seven students?

      44. Formula: $z =$ _____

      45. Answer: _____

D. Computation:

Directions: Use the data given to answer questions 46-50.

_____ 46. Student A got a raw score of 124 on the ABC test ($M = 100, S = 16$). What would be his z score?

_____ 47. Student B got a raw score of 122.5 on the XYZ test ($M = 100, S = 15$). What would be his z score?

_____ 48. Which student — A or B — has the higher score?

_____ 49. What percent would be between a z score of -2 and a z score of $+1$, assuming a normal distribution?

_____ 50. An individual obtained a raw score of 62 on a test whose $M = 50$ and $S = 10$. What T score would he have to obtain to stay at the same z-score level on a test whose $M = 100$ and $S = 15$?

Use the data given below to answer questions 51-55.

Student	Test 1 X	z_1	Test 2 Y	z_2
A	6	1.5	7	1.0
B	5	1.0	6	0.5
C	3	0	2	-1.5
D	4	0.5	7	1.0
E	0	-1.5	5	0
F	0	-1.5	5	0
G	3	0	2	-1.5
H	1	-1.0	3	-1.0
I	3	0	5	0
J	5	1.0	8	1.5
	$M = 3$		$M = 5$	
	$S = 2$		$S = 2$	

_____ 51. Graph the above data and tell whether there is a correlation or not.

_____ 52. Calculate r using the z-*score* method.

_____ 53. Calculate r using the *raw-score* method.

_____ 54. What is the sign of the value found for r?

_____ 55. Interpret the value (index) you found for the correlation.

E. Completion:

Directions: For questions 56-70, write the correct answer to each question on the line provided.

56. The most widely used measure of variability is the _____ _____.

57. For a large number of measures, a frequency polygon usually takes the shape of a _____.

58. For **z** scores we usually assign the numerical value _____
to the central point of the curve and _____ for each
standard deviation.

59. Numbers to the right of the central point in a **z** score distribution are assigned _____ values, and number to the
left are assigned _____ values.

If **M** = 6 and **S** = 2, what are the **z** scores corresponding to the
following raw scores?

60. For raw score 8, **z** = _____ .

61. For raw score 2, **z** = _____ .

62. For raw score 7, **z** = _____ .

63. For raw score 10, **z** =. _____ .

For a normal distribution, what percents would fall between the
following **z** scores?

64. Between **z** = −1 and **z** = −2, % = _____ .

65. Between **z** = 0 and **z** = 1, % = _____ .

66. Between **z** = 2 and **z** = 3, % = _____ .

67. Between **z** = 1 and **z** = 2, % = _____ .

Define each of the following as briefly and accurately as you can.

68. **z** score _____

_____

69. correlation; **r** _____

_____

70. List four major advantages or characteristics of the Pearson
Product-Moment technique.

a. _____

b. _____

c. _____

d. _____

Appendix D

Answers to Test: MUST Parts I and II

A.

1. c
2. b
3. a
4. a
5. c
6. b
7. c
8. d
9. b
10. d
11. b
12. a
13. d
14. d
15. c
16. a
17. c
18. a
19. a
20. a
21. d

B.

22. b
23. i
24. h
25. c
26. g
27. d
28. f
29. e
30. l
31. o
32. n
33. p
34. q
35. r
36. a
37. t

C.

38. $\dfrac{\Sigma X}{N}$

39. 5

40. $X - M$

41. $-3; -2; -1; 0; 1; 2; 3$

42. $\sqrt{\dfrac{\Sigma x^2}{N}}$

43. 2

44. $\dfrac{X - M}{S}$

45. $-1.5; -1.0; -0.5; 0; 0.5;$ $1.0; 1.5$

46. $z = 1.5$

Computation:

$$z = \frac{X - M}{S}$$

$$= \frac{124 - 100}{16} = \frac{24}{16} = 1.5$$

47. $z = 1.5$

Computation:

$$z = \frac{X - M}{S}$$

$$= \frac{122.5 - 100}{15} = \frac{22.5}{15} = 1.5$$

48. Student B got the higher raw score, but both scored at the same z score level. This does not mean, however, that the scores are interchangeable since the norms for the two tests are different. It does mean that in relation to the mean and standard deviation for the test, the raw scores for the two students are about equal.

49. 82%

50. $T = 118$

Computation:

$$z = \frac{X - M}{S} \qquad\qquad T = M + zS$$

$$= \frac{62 - 50}{10} \qquad\qquad = 100 + (1.2)15$$

$$= 1.2 \qquad\qquad\qquad = 118$$

51. Yes, there appears to be a positive correlation.

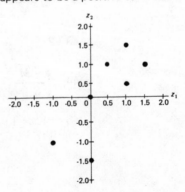

52. $r = 0.50$
   Computation:

$$r = \frac{\Sigma z_1 z_2}{N}$$

$$= \frac{5}{10}$$

$$= 0.50$$

53. $r = 0.50$
   Computation:

$$r = \frac{N\Sigma XY - \Sigma X \Sigma Y}{\sqrt{N\Sigma X^2 - (\Sigma X)^2}\sqrt{N\Sigma Y^2 - (\Sigma Y)^2}}$$

$$= \frac{(10)(170) - (30)(50)}{\sqrt{10(130) - (30)^2}\sqrt{10(290) - (50)^2}}$$

$$= \frac{1700 - 1500}{\sqrt{1300 - 900}\sqrt{2900 - 2500}}$$

$$= \frac{200}{(20)(20)}$$

$$= \frac{200}{400}$$

$$= 0.50$$

54. This r is positive.

55. This is a positive correlation; there is, therefore, a relationship between scores on the two tests.

56. standard deviation

57. normal curve

58. zero . . . one.

59. positive . . . negative.

60. +1.0

61. −2.0

62. +0.5

63. +2.0

64. 14

65. 34

66. 2

67. 14

68. *z* scores represent the number of standard deviations a raw score is away from the mean in either direction.

69. Correlation technique provides a number as an index of the relationship between sets of scores; *r* is Pearson's Product-Moment correlation coefficient.

70. a. It is independent of the original measurement units.

    b. It is independent of the number of scores.

    c. The sign of the index number indicates whether there is a positive or a negative correlation.

    d. The numerical value indicates the relative strength of the correlation.

Appendix E

Case 1: Test Interpretation of the STS Educational Development Series (EDS)*

(In this protocol **C** refers to the counselor and **S** refers to the students involved in the small group interpretation.)

C: "Recently you took the *Educational Development Series* (EDS). Do you remember the test?"

S: "Uh-huh. They're the ones we took in the cafeteria."

S: "The same kind we took the other times — when we were in the ninth grade, you know."

C: "Yes, this is the *Educational Development Series.* We administer them to Grades 3, 6, 9 and 11 as a part of the State-County Testing program. Do you remember the areas of ability or achievement measured by these tests? (Shows list.) Non-Verbal Ability, Verbal Ability, Reading, English, Mathematics, Science, The U. S. A. in the World, and your ability in Solving Everyday Problems. Do you remember the kinds of questions you were asked?"

S: (Several comments.)

C: "Let's look at some of the kinds of questions asked. (Shows them booklets.) Look at the math portion: It asked, 'If you had $5.00 and went to the store and bought 6 apples at a nickel apiece and 7 oranges at 10 cents apiece, how much change would you have?' This type of thing made up the mathematics part of the test. In the reading test, you read a paragraph and then were asked questions about what went on in the paragraph. The English test concerned punctuation — where there would be a sentence and you would have to punctuate it correctly. Do you remember all that?"

S: "Uh-huh. We have had other tests like this. They're really hard."

S: "How did our scores compare with others?"

C: "This is what the test interpretation is all about. Do you have any concept of what the normal curve is? You know, it's shaped like this." (Draws curve and indicates three areas: 'Low,'

---

*We are indebted to Ferguson Meadows, Jr. (**C**), Stonewall Jackson High School, and a group of students (**S**) for the use of this transcribed report of a small group test interpretation. The EDS, published by Scholastic Testing Service, was administered to all of the students in Grade 11 as a part of the West Virginia State-County Testing Program.

'Average,' and 'High.') "Now all of the scores of all people will fall between this point (lowest) and this point (highest). The majority of the scores will fall in this area here. (Indicates 'Average' range.) If you didn't know anything at all about yourself or the test, where would you guess your score would fall?"

S: "Average."

C: "Yes, most scores would be somewhere within the average range. If you took the test again today, would you score *exactly* like you did last time?"

S: "No, not exactly. I would remember more."

S: "I might not guess the same way."

S: (Other comments.)

C: "You're right. If you took the test again, say a hundred times, we know the scores would spread out around the score you got last time — like this. (Indicates variation by placing X's on curve.) But, we can be 95% sure that it would fall between two points — say here, and here (Draws band to enclose most of the X's.) This is what we tell you when we interpret your score on a standardized test — that if you took the test over and over, it would probably be somewhere within a certain area. We call this a band. So your scores will be interpreted as a band."

S: "It's like guessing that a score is average — the band is the same way, if we took it again?"

S: (Brief comments indicating agreement and understanding.)

C: "That's right. Now, think about the day you took the test: Do you recall if you were sick or feeling bad that day, or was it a pretty good day?"

S: "It was raining."

S: "I was so sleepy."

S: "Dead day."

C: "Kind of a dull day?"

S: "Yeah, it was."

C: "Do you think this might have influenced the way you performed on the test?"

S: "Yeah, definitely."

S: "Sure."

S: "Definitely."

S: "The atmosphere, you know. We were pretty stuffy in there."

C: "Kind of a dull day — but apparently not different enough, or nothing unusual happened, to keep you from performing as you usually would?"

S: (General agreement.)

C: "Okay. What I'm going to do now is give you all a sheet . . . and if you look at the sheet (Figure 79), you'll notice . . . go ahead and put your name at the top of it . . . it has on it the various areas which were on the test such as Non-Verbal, Verbal, Science, Mathematics, etc. So, what I want you to do, . . . okay, we'll do it one at a time and we will read each particular ability or skill that we are going to measure, and you mark on the paper how you think you did in that particular area. So let's start with Non-Verbal. I'm going to read it to you and you read it to yourself. Non-Verbal — Here we're talking about your ability to solve problems involving different kinds of pictures. I think you probably remember that portion of the test. So go ahead and mark on your paper what you think you scored or whereabouts you think you scored."

S: "How do you want us . . . "

S: "How many numbers do you put in?"

C: "Just circle the number. If it's in between, just put a circle between the two."

S: "Okay."

C: "Okay, the next one is Verbal Ability. So go ahead and read it. This is your ability to solve problems involving different kinds of words. (Pause.) Okay, the next area is Reading. This is your ability to read different kinds of stories quickly and accurately. (Pause.) The next area is English. Here they were concerned with your ability to use the English language correctly, your grammar, capitalization, punctuation, and spelling. That's the one we talked about a few minutes ago. (Pause.) The next sheet shows the mathematics portion. This dealt with your ability to work with numbers and to solve problems using numbers. (Pause.) The next area is Science. This tried to find out how much knowledge you had concerning the important facts of science and your ability to solve problems in science. Okay, did everybody get that marked?"

S: "Uh-huh."

C: "The next area is the U. S. A. in the World. Now this is your knowledge of facts about your country — its geography, its history, and its relations with other countries. (Pause.) Okay, now the last area is Solving Everyday Problems. This is your knowledge of important facts about schools and jobs, and your ability to solve practical problems outside the school. (Pause.) Okay, has everybody got it marked now? I want you to keep that sheet, and I will give you a sheet with your actual scores — using bands — on it, and I want you to transfer that score off

Educational Development Series
Test Interpretation Form

Name: _____

Date: _____

Non-Verbal — Your ability to solve problems involving different
            kinds of pictures

My ability is somewhat lower than most	My ability is about that of most (average)	My ability is somewhat higher than most
1 2 3	4 5 6	7 8 9

Verbal Ability — Your ability to solve problems involving different
                kinds of words

My ability is somewhat lower than most	My ability is about that of most (average)	My ability is somewhat higher than most
1 2 3	4 5 6	7 8 9

Reading — Your ability to read different kinds of stories quickly
          and accurately

My ability is somewhat lower than most	My ability is about that of most (average)	My ability is somewhat higher than most
1 2 3	4 5 6	7 8 9

English — Your ability to use the English language correctly —
          grammar, capitalization, punctuation, and spelling

My ability is somewhat lower than most	My ability is about that of most (average)	My ability is somewhat higher than most
1 2 3	4 5 6	7 8 9

Fig. 79. STS-EDS Test Interpretation Form

140

Mathematics — Your ability to work with numbers and to solve problems using numbers

My ability is somewhat lower than most	My ability is about that of most (average)	My ability is somewhat higher than most
1 2 3	4 5 6	7 8 9

Science — Your knowledge of important facts in science, and your ability to solve problems in science

My ability is somewhat lower than most	My ability is about that of most (average)	My ability is somewhat higher than most
1 2 3	4 5 6	7 8 9

The U.S.A. in the World — Your knowledge of facts about your country — its geography, its history, and its relations with other countries

My ability is somewhat lower than most	My ability is about that of most (average)	My ability is somewhat higher than most
1 2 3	4 5 6	7 8 9

Solving Everyday Problems — Your knowledge of important facts about schools and jobs, and your ability to solve practical problems outside of school

My ability is somewhat lower than most	My ability is about that of most (average)	My ability is somewhat higher than most
1 2 3	4 5 6	7 8 9

Fig. 79. Continued

the one you just marked on the sheet." (Hands out EDS Test Interpretation Forms for each student — Figures 80, 81, 82, 83.)

C: "For example on the first one, Non-Verbal, if you marked yourself a three on the first page, then mark a three on the other one. Okay? Understand? Just transfer the score from one sheet to the other sheet. Go ahead and do that for all the scores. (Pause.) Is everyone finished?"

S: "Uh-huh" (general agreement).

C: "Compare your two sets of scores — the one you estimated, and the band. Did you score pretty much as you thought you would?"

S: "Most of 'em."

S: "Yeah."

S: "Uh-huh."

S: "I think."

S: "I scored less on some of them."

C: "Which ones?"

S: "A lot are less. Like on Non-Verbal Ability, Reading, Science, and U.S.A. in the World. Well, maybe I didn't miss them very much."

C: "So you estimated a little bit better than you scored?"

S: "Right."

C: "How would you account for that? Kinda surprise yourself?"

S: "Yes, I think I did surprise myself."

C: "Okay, what about you, Chris? You started to say something about . . . "

S: "It's mostly okay all the way thru except on the last one — Solving Everyday Problems."

C: "You marked yourself higher than you actually scored?"

S: "Uh-huh."

C: "Why did you say you think you did that?"

S: " 'Cause on that test I just sorta — they were — I don't know, I just sorta went down and marked them. I didn't really read them."

C: "You didn't really put yourself into them?"

S: "I didn't think about them. In everyday life I can solve problems better."

C: "You said it was a pretty bad day. It was kind of dreary outside. That might have affected your attitude toward taking the test?"

S: "Definitely."

C: "Did these scores help you make any decisions about your future plans, going to college, getting a job, or whatever?"

S: "No. My scores and estimates are the same."

S: "Do they help us or do they hurt us?"

C: "Do they help you make any decisions about . . . "

S: "No, I think we're wasting time sitting here."

S: "Me too."

C: "You're saying . . . "

S: "That unless somebody *else* is going to see what we scored — if we rate average, below average, or above average — to help us, then it doesn't make any difference what we score. That would be the only thing it would be good for, I would think."

S: "I think that it might tell us that — like if you're working up to your ability — like, I'm high on the test, and in class I didn't work up to what I should and got low grades."

C: "Chris, you're saying that you felt you pretty much know what you're going to do anyway, so that test really wasn't that valuable to you?"

S: "That's right. Only I didn't try very much on that *one* part."

C: "You feel you could have done better if you had really tried? Does this information help you in making any decisions about your education, or your work?"

S: "No. I guess I'm mostly average. I'll probably have to work hard if I go to college."

S: "I scored about average on all of it except for Non-Verbal. I'm not sure now, what that means."

S: "I marked mine higher than I scored — or at the high end of the band. I always make good grades."

S: "Yes."

C: "While you were within the band, you're wondering why you scored that low?"

S: "I study lots — maybe that's the reason."

C: "For the most part, you all scored just about like you thought you would?"

S: "Uh-huh."

C: "Any questions? (Pause.) Okay. Take the sheets with your reported scores on them home with you and show them to your parents. If you or they have any questions, please feel free to make an appointment to discuss them with me."

Legend: ⭕ Student's Self-Estimate

▨▨▨ Obtained score to include approximately ± 2 SEM

Name: __A__

Date: _____

Non-Verbal — Your ability to solve problems involving different kinds of pictures

My ability is somewhat lower than most	My ability is about that of most (average)	My ability is somewhat higher than most
▨1▨ 2 ▨3▨	**④** 5 6	7 8 9

Verbal Ability — Your ability to solve problems involving different kinds of words

My ability is somewhat lower than most	My ability is about that of most (average)	My ability is somewhat higher than most
1 ▨2▨ 3	▨④ 5 6▨	7 8 9

Reading — Your ability to read different kinds of stories quickly and accurately

My ability is somewhat lower than most	My ability is about that of most (average)	My ability is somewhat higher than most
1 ▨2 3	4 ⑤ 6▨	7 8 9

English — Your ability to use the English language correctly — grammar, capitalization, punctuation, and spelling

My ability is somewhat lower than most	My ability is about that of most (average)	My ability is somewhat higher than most
▨1 2 3▨ 4	**⑤** 6	7 8 9

Fig. 80. STS-EDS Interpretation for Student A

Mathematics — Your ability to work with numbers and to solve problems using numbers

My ability is somewhat lower than most	My ability is about that of most (average)	My ability is somewhat higher than most
1 2 3 4 5 6		7 8 9

Science — Your knowledge of important facts in science, and your ability to solve problems in science

My ability is somewhat lower than most	My ability is about that of most (average)	My ability is somewhat higher than most
1 2 3 4 5 6		7 8 9

The U.S.A. in the World — Your knowledge of facts about your country — its geography, its history, and its relations with other countries

My ability is somewhat lower than most	My ability is about that of most (average)	My ability is somewhat higher than most
1 2 3 4 5 6		7 8 9

Solving Everyday Problems — Your knowledge of important facts about schools and jobs, and your ability to solve practical problems outside of school

My ability is somewhat lower than most	My ability is about that of most (average)	My ability is somewhat higher than most
1 2 3 4 5 6		7 8 9

Fig. 80. Continued

145

Legend: ⃝ Student's Self-Estimate

▨▨▨ Obtained score to include approximately ± 2 SEM

Name: **B**

Date: _____

Non-Verbal — Your ability to solve problems involving different kinds of pictures

My ability is somewhat lower than most	My ability is about that of most (average)	My ability is somewhat higher than most
▨ 1 ▨ 2 ▨ 3 ▨ 4 **⑤** 6	7 8 9

Verbal Ability — Your ability to solve problems involving different kinds of words

My ability is somewhat lower than most	My ability is about that of most (average)	My ability is somewhat higher than most
▨ 1 ▨ 2 ▨ 3 ⊛4 5 6	7 8 9

Reading — Your ability to read different kinds of stories quickly and accurately

My ability is somewhat lower than most	My ability is about that of most (average)	My ability is somewhat higher than most
▨ 1 ▨ 2 ▨ 3 ▨ 4 ⊛5 6	7 8 9

English — Your ability to use the English language correctly — grammar, capitalization, punctuation, and spelling

My ability is somewhat lower than most	My ability is about that of most (average)	My ability is somewhat higher than most
▨ 1 ▨ 2 ▨ 3 ⊛4 5 6	7 8 9

Fig. 81. STS-EDS Interpretation for Student B

146

Mathematics — Your ability to work with numbers and to solve
problems using numbers

My ability is somewhat lower than most	My ability is about that of most (average)		My ability is somewhat higher than most	
▨1▨2▨3▨4 ⑤ 6			7 8 9	

Science — Your knowledge of important facts in science, and your
ability to solve problems in science

My ability is somewhat lower than most	My ability is about that of most (average)		My ability is somewhat higher than most	
▨1▨2▨3 ④ 5 6			7 8 9	

The U.S.A. in the World — Your knowledge of facts about your
country — its geography, its history,
and its relations with other countries

My ability is somewhat lower than most	My ability is about that of most (average)		My ability is somewhat higher than most	
▨1▨2▨3▨4 ⑤ 6			7 8 9	

Solving Everyday Problems — Your knowledge of important facts
about schools and jobs, and your
ability to solve practical problems
outside of school

My ability is somewhat lower than most	My ability is about that of most (average)		My ability is somewhat higher than most	
▨1▨2▨3 ④ 5 6			7 8 9	

Fig. 81. Continued

147

Legend: ◯ Student's Self-Estimate

⨯⨯⨯ Obtained score to include approximately ± 2 SEM

Name: **C**

Date: _____

Non-Verbal — Your ability to solve problems involving different kinds of pictures

My ability is somewhat lower than most	My ability is about that of most (average)	My ability is somewhat higher than most
1 2 3	4 5 6	⑦ 8 9

Verbal Ability — Your ability to solve problems involving different kinds of words

My ability is somewhat lower than most	My ability is about that of most (average)	My ability is somewhat higher than most
1 2 3	4 ⑤ 6	7 8 9

Reading — Your ability to read different kinds of stories quickly and accurately

My ability is somewhat lower than most	My ability is about that of most (average)	My ability is somewhat higher than most
1 2 3	④ 5 6	7 8 9

English — Your ability to use the English language correctly — grammar, capitalization, punctuation, and spelling

My ability is somewhat lower than most	My ability is about that of most (average)	My ability is somewhat higher than most
1 2 3	4 5 ⑥	7 8 9

Fig. 82. STS-EDS Interpretation for Student C

148

Mathematics — Your ability to work with numbers and to solve problems using numbers

My ability is somewhat lower than most	My ability is about that of most (average)	My ability is somewhat higher than most
1 2 **3** **4** 5 **⑥** **7** 8 9		

Science — Your knowledge of important facts in science, and your ability to solve problems in science

My ability is somewhat lower than most	My ability is about that of most (average)	My ability is somewhat higher than most
1 2 **3** **④** 5 6 **7** 8 9		

The U.S.A. in the World — Your knowledge of facts about your country — its geography, its history, and its relations with other countries

My ability is somewhat lower than most	My ability is about that of most (average)	My ability is somewhat higher than most
1 2 **3** **4** **⑤** 6 **7** 8 9		

Solving Everyday Problems — Your knowledge of important facts about schools and jobs, and your ability to solve practical problems outside of school

My ability is somewhat lower than most	My ability is about that of most (average)	My ability is somewhat higher than most
1 2 **3** **4** **5** **6** **⑦** 8 9		

Fig. 82. Continued

Legend: ⭕ Student's Self-Estimate

⬚⬚⬚ Obtained score to include approximately ± 2 SEM

Name: **D**

Date: _____

Non-Verbal — Your ability to solve problems involving different kinds of pictures

My ability is somewhat lower than most	My ability is about that of most (average)	My ability is somewhat higher than most

1　2　3　4　⑤　6　7　8　9

Verbal Ability — Your ability to solve problems involving different kinds of words

My ability is somewhat lower than most	My ability is about that of most (average)	My ability is somewhat higher than most

1　2　3　④　5　6　7　8　9

Reading — Your ability to read different kinds of stories quickly and accurately

My ability is somewhat lower than most	My ability is about that of most (average)	My ability is somewhat higher than most

1　2　3　4　5　⑥　7　8　9

English — Your ability to use the English language correctly — grammar, capitalization, punctuation, and spelling

My ability is somewhat lower than most	My ability is about that of most (average)	My ability is somewhat higher than most

1　2　3　4　⑤　6　7　8　9

Fig. 83. STS-EDS Interpretation for Student D

150

Mathematics — Your ability to work with numbers and to solve problems using numbers

My ability is somewhat lower than most	My ability is about that of most (average)	My ability is somewhat higher than most
1 ② 3 4 5 6	7 8 9	

Science — Your knowledge of important facts in science, and your ability to solve problems in science

My ability is somewhat lower than most	My ability is about that of most (average)	My ability is somewhat higher than most
1 2 3 ④ 5 6	7 8 9	

The U.S.A. in the World — Your knowledge of facts about your country — its geography, its history, and its relations with other countries

My ability is somewhat lower than most	My ability is about that of most (average)	My ability is somewhat higher than most
1 2 3 ④ 5 6	7 8 9	

Solving Everyday Problems — Your knowledge of important facts about schools and jobs, and your ability to solve practical problems outside of school

My ability is somewhat lower than most	My ability is about that of most (average)	My ability is somewhat higher than most
1 2 3 4 5 6	⑦ 8 9	

Fig. 83. Continued

151

Appendix F

Case 2: Interpretation of GATB*

(In this protocol **C** refers to Mr. Phillips, the counselor, and **R** refers to Roger, the client.)

C: "Do you recall the name of the test you took last Friday, Roger?"

R: "Not particularly, no."

C: "It was the *General Aptitude Test Battery* (GATB). Last week I think you mentioned that you had an *aptitude* test when you went into the military service?"

R: "Yes."

C: "So, maybe you were a little familiar with what it would be like. Was there anything particular that stood out in your mind as far as any parts of the test?"

R: "No, nothing, as far as that goes. (Pause) What is this test supposed to determine anyway — what you are skilled in or something like that?"

C: "Right, this more or less tries to predict your potential or to *detect* your ability to do certain types of work or to endure certain types of training. Of course, there is no one test that says that you *can* do this or says you *can't* do that. There are other things to consider too. For example, maybe you studied some subjects a whole lot or something like this."

R: "Un-huh, some things I liked — some I didn't."

C: "This test compares how you scored on this test with other people who took the test. (Draws normal curve on paper while Roger looks on.) What I want to do is explain this . . . (Pause.) While you were in school, did you have a teacher who discussed test scores using a normal distribution like this?"

R: "No."

C: "Well, this is called a normal distribution. All of the test scores — for everybody who took the test — all of the test scores fall along this line (indicates base line). For example, on this test, all of the scores are somewhere from this point (left end) to

---

*We are indebted to John Phillips, Employment Counselor, Beckley, West Virginia, for the use of this transcribed report of an actual test interpretation following his training in the SELF procedures presented in Part II of this Manual. Only the identifying data have been altered.

153

this point (right end). Most scores fell somewhere along the middle. Your score fell somewhere along this line . . . If you took this test again, next week, say, do you think your score would be the same? The exact score?"

R: "You mean if I had the same material and everything?"

C: "Un-huh."

R: "No, I wouldn't think so. It seems like you'd remember what it said."

C: "What you are saying is that it could be as high as this (indicates higher range) because you'd recall some of the material. Or it could be as high as this (indicates highest range). If you were not feeling very good the day when you took the test, it might be here. Or put it around the other way, say you took it yesterday or Friday, uh, say you took it next week and you were not feeling very good, how do you think that would affect your score?"

R: "There would be a lot of conditions in there that you'd have to look at."

C: "It could even be lower the next time you took it?"

R: "Uh-huh."

C: "Or it could be the same or higher or even lower." (Indicates possible range by placing X's along base line.)

C: "When I go over your actual test or test scores, because of this, you know — because your test performance could fluctuate and does — I'll give your test scores in the form of a band; and I'll say you are somewhere between here and here, instead of saying you're right here — at an exact number — because of these and other factors.

"This band takes care of what we call 'standard error of measurement.' So with the use of a band, uh, we're pretty certain that your scores are somewhere between these points. The research done shows that if you took it next week or the week after it wouldn't be the same, but it would fall within the band anyway."

C: "Now, as far as the normal curve, most people fall between these two marks here (indicates average range), at least 68% of the people. Now, let's use the 'G' scores, General Learning Ability, as an example. Let's say that you are average. That's like saying, 'I learn the same as most people.' Now, going to the right, you could say, 'I learn more, or more easily, than most people.' Uh, still going a little bit higher to the right, as high as you can go, really, you are saying, 'I learn much more easily.' Now coming back to the left of average here, or where most people fall, we could say that learning is more difficult for you than it is for the average. And coming on·down, we could say *much more* difficult."

C: "Now, if I didn't know a thing about you and I didn't know about your school work or anything else, if I were to make a guess about your test score — just from this curve here — what do you think I would estimate?"

R: "Well, I don't know, to start off with this here, you'd put it right in here, wouldn't you, the average?"

C: "Okay, we know that most people would fall within the average range so we would say that most of the time with most people we would come within this estimate. We would say that 68% of the people fall within here."

R: "Pretty good odds to work on, isn't it?"

C: "Pretty good odds, uh-huh."

R: "Let me ask you a question about that test. What relation does this have? You know, you take this test and you're placed sorta in that category there — what's the purpose of finding it and taking the test, you know, in relationship, you know, to counseling?"

C: "Well, uh, in your instance, you've been out of service five or six months, and I think you told me just traveling and taking it easy. Uh, you've decided you have to go to work and want to go to work, you couldn't come up with any stated interest, as far as what kind of work you wanted."

R: "That's true."

C: "Uh, you see this interest check list, different jobs you see, you marked whether you liked them or disliked them; and we still didn't come up with anything that seemed interesting. So at that time I told you about the aptitude test, and by taking this we can predict different jobs by putting these different aptitudes together — and maybe by doing this and going through these interpretations, maybe this will bring out some job interest."

R: "Is this part of the standard process, you know, all this?"

C: "Uh-huh. If you hadn't wanted to take the test, I wouldn't have given it to you. And some people just don't want to take the test. Does that answer your question?"

R: "Yes, I understand it now."

C: "Now, this is what we'll do: The test measures lots of areas and I'd like to go over each one with you. And then before I'll give you the actual test scores in this type of band, I want you to estimate where you think you scored, and then we'll take what you estimate for your scores and compare them to your regular score."

R: "O.K."

C: "Now here's a description of the nine areas on which you were tested. G — General Learning Ability, Verbal Aptitude and so on. Now over here to the right, it tells you what part of the test actually measured this area — like the general learning ability which is measured by part three; part four — vocabulary; and part six — arithmetic reasoning. And these three made up a score — the General Learning Ability score. Now you go ahead and look over these and, uh, there's a description for each one. Go ahead and look them over and get an idea what they measure and we'll discuss them a little bit."

R: "All right." (Pause.)

C: "As far as the General Learning Ability, uh, say, you more or less use this in school or something like this. What do you think would relate to general learning?"

R: "I don't hardly agree with that there, where it says *closely related* to doing well in school. Is that supposed to fit in there? I mean, like, you know, if you didn't do so well in school, according to me, the way it reads here, your General Learning Ability would be poor, right?"

C: "Let me see if I get what you are saying. Are you saying that maybe you had the learning ability but you didn't put out in school, you don't think that would be related?"

R: "Yeh."

C: "I agree with you. You're right. You could have all the ability in the world, but if you don't train yourself and use it you wouldn't do well in school. So what you're saying, just having the ability doesn't mean you are going to be a success in some kind of training."

R: "You have to try, too."

C: "How about the Verbal Aptitude. Again, you can relate this back to your school as far as English class."

R: "No, I don't have it. You know, it's a, you know, if you relate everything back to when you were in school, you know, I've been out almost six years and it's hard to, you know, just to know what you did then."

C: "Well, when you estimate the scores you may compare them with what you think you could do. You say you didn't try in school?"

R: "No, I didn't."

C: "So, when you estimate your General Learning Ability, you should consider that you didn't try in school, shouldn't you? You may have average grades in some classes and low grades in some. It may have been that you didn't study?"

R: "Right, I guess so."

C: "Let's see, here. This chart is marked off like the normal curve — the middle area is average. Let's go ahead and, uh, check one of these areas. You may refer back to the definition for the parts that make up the test, and just estimate what you think you got on the test before we go over the actual test results. Put an X or a check mark where you think you scored."

R: "You mean I could just put an X on the line where I think I score — like that?"

C: "Yes, go ahead and mark them. Here, for example, on the first one, do you consider yourself average, at the top of average, below average, or above average?"

R: "I see what you are doing, but I still don't understand, you know, the purpose behind me filling out what I think it will be."

C: "It is just a way of interpreting the test scores, and uh, the thing is that most people estimate their scores pretty close to what the scores actually are. This means, uh, putting it in these terms, that most people usually know their ability."
(Roger estimates scores.)

R: "What do you want me to do now?"

C: "Now, we will see what your actual test scores are. Take this sheet (hands Roger sheet with bands reported), and then what you estimated, and mark over the top here at the same place you marked on the first sheet."

R: "You want this just transferred to this one?"

C: "Right."
(Roger does as instructed.)

C: "There's hardly any of these where your estimate falls within the band. However, you could more or less say that you guessed your scores pretty close to actually what you got. Did you score about what you expected?"

R: "No."

C: "Looks like you missed?"

R: "Sure did. Missed it quite a bit. I got two of them right though, or pretty close." (Laugh.)

C: "What you did, say, you estimated your scores quite a bit lower than what you got."

R: "Seems that way according to the chart, doesn't it?"

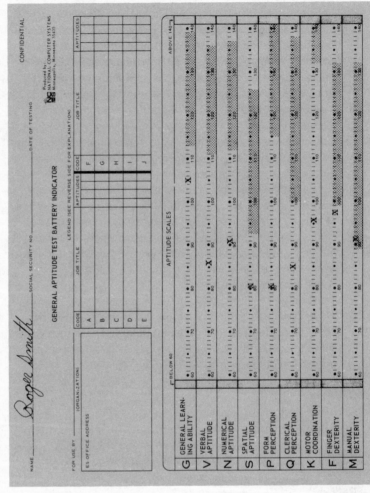

Fig. 84 GATB Interpretation for Roger Smith

158

C: "What do you think that tells you?"

R: "Well, if it tells anything at all, it might mean that I'm under-estimating things, ability-wise."

C: "If the test is valid, it might mean that you have higher ability than you actually think you have."

R: "That's what it looks like, doesn't it."

C: "What you're saying then, is that you have the ability, but don't apply yourself. I think you used school for an example a while ago, particularly for *G,* you know, General Learning Ability, to estimate how you scored. Your problem is, I gather, that you didn't do real well in school?"

R: "No, I didn't. Well, I did reasonably well until about the tenth grade, or something like that, and then I sorta lost interest in school."

C: "You lost interest?"

R: "Yeah, I didn't care much for it after that."

C: "You found the subjects too easy or too hard at that time?"

R: "Nah, I got along all right in 'em. I just come to the point that I, you know, just didn't care whether I made it or not. It just didn't seem important to me at that time."

C: "But you just went ahead and stayed with it and graduated?"

R: "Well, yeah, just graduated."

C: "You just more or less did enough to get by with?"

R: "True enough."

C: "Well, how do you think you can use these test results as far as, uh, well, jobs?"

R: "I don't know, you're the counselor, you will have to tell me about it. I believe, see how I apply to it and everything."

C: "I'll tell you one thing you can say, you know, just from looking at the test results — that your learning ability is higher than that required for the things you have been thinking about, although your job interest has not been implemented anyway."

R: "That's true. I don't know, I am just having trouble deciding just what I do want to do — want to get into, like, you know, I've had two years in the Army considering — like what I want to do when I get out. And here I've taken almost another year and I still haven't decided, so I don't know."

C: "So it's real hard for you to make a decision like that."

R: "I might be prime material for West Virginia's Welfare Program if I keep this attitude."

C: "You think your attitude keeps you from deciding?"

R: "I really don't know what it is. I've thought quite a bit about it and I don't know. My interests just seem so limited, I guess. I don't know what to limit it to though."

C: "Are you afraid to make some kind of a decision — afraid it will be something you won't like?"

R: "Yeah, I guess, more or less, that's what it could be."

C: "What do you think those test results tell you as far as even college level training?"

R: "Well, I've thought about college, but you know I told you that I didn't do well in school and I really don't have the background. You know I'd probably have to have extra training and everything else to even get into college. I don't think I'd be able to do the work."

C: "You don't think you could apply yourself and really hit the books and do college level work? If you wouldn't do this, you probably wouldn't be successful at it."

R: "I'd be so far behind, I wouldn't really know how to start about it."

C: "Well, what was your average in school, Roger?"

R: "It would only be about average, probably a low average."

C: "You failed some subjects in high school?"

R: "Yeh, well I'd failed maybe a nine weeks in something I didn't care much about. Then I could bring it back up, try a little harder, and bring it back up and pass it the next time."

C: "You studied when you thought you were going to fail the class?"

R: "Yeh, you know a little spark would get throwed in there, or something, and I'd take right off."

C: "Would you consider yourself always having trouble making a decision on a job?"

R: "No, not really, I don't know. I just can't understand myself, you know, why I can't find some kind of job interest."

C: "Have you explored a lot of different kind of occupations — found out a lot of information about them?"

R: "Yeah, I've checked around pretty extensively."

C: "You'd like to tell me some of the jobs you've thought about?"

R: "I haven't narrowed it down to anything specific like that — you know, in the broad sense of the word, checked into things. I don't know, I guess about the only thing I could do is to, well, is to just check around. And maybe I'll run across something that I do like and then just try it, as far as I know. It doesn't sound like I'd make a very steady employee anywhere, but until I find something that's the only thing I can do."

C: "I can suggest something that may be some help to you. This book is related to job aptitudes — you scored higher than the required scores in all the jobs listed. In addition, you can start looking through this at *specific* job titles. I can let you use this. I also have an *Occupational Outlook Handbook*. You may have used this when you were in high school, I don't know."

R: "I think I recall it, I don't know."

C: "It has an index in the back, an alphabetical listing of jobs. Do you have a particular job in mind? You can go to this book and get what the requirements are for it, how much education it requires, the exact job earnings, working conditions, and everything. And I think, from just talking to you, you may need something like this."

R: "I'm going to need something, I believe, I don't know what it is." (Laugh.)

C: "This is something as far as jobs are concerned — you're going to have to decide for yourself. Now, I can let you look over some of these today, or you can come back if you want to this evening. What I would like for you to do is to look over these and then I'd like to talk to you again."

R: "I don't think I really have time this evening. Maybe the next time I come in."

C: "What day is that when you sign up for your unemployment?"

R: "On Mondays."

C: "You could make an appointment for Monday. I could give you one of these offices here. I'll give you the books and you can sit down and start going over them any time you want to."

R: "If it will be all right with you, I'll come in next Monday, then."

Appendix G
Reprinted with permission from
Exceptional Children, Volume 38,
Number 1, September, 1971.

STERLING L. ROSS, JR.
HENRY G. DeYOUNG
JULIUS S. COHEN

Confrontation: Special Education Placement and the Law

Abstract: Recently, suits have been brought against public schools for placing certain children in special classes for the educable mentally retarded. Through the courts parents are challenging the administration and use of standardized tests, placement procedures, and the effectiveness and the harmful impact of special class programing. Special educators are urged to initiate immediate reform in testing and placement procedures or there is a likelihood that changes will be imposed by the courts. The possibility of punitive damages may stimulate these changes.

In the nation's public schools, classes for the educable mentally retarded have unwittingly become burial grounds for many children from environments that have not prepared them for the demands of the schools. The educational system has consistently ignored pleas for change to make school experience more relevant to children who may be neither highly motivated nor achievement oriented or who come from culturally different backgrounds. In an effort to make the educational system reponsive to the children's needs, concerned parents have turned to the courts. In recent years a groundswell of litigation has arisen, attacking the criteria currently used to label and place children of racial and cultural minorities in special programs. Such intense judicial activity has important implications for educators concerned with the

seriousness of the present situation and highlights the need for immediate change.

The Arguments

The following arguments are levied most often against current placement procedures.

For many children, testing does not accurately measure their learning ability. Intelligence tests are generally standardized on white, middle class student populations, are heavily verbal, and contain questions more easily answerable by white, middle class students. These three factors coalesce to produce IQ scores which are based primarily on cultural and/or socioeconomic backgrounds of the students and are not a true indication of learning ability. The tests discriminate against children of racial and cultural minorities and are therefore in violation of the equal protection clause of the 14th Amendment to the United States Constitution.

The administration of tests is often performed incompetently. Even if proper testing instruments existed, many of the present public school personnel are not adequately trained to administer the tests nor qualified to interpret the results prop-

STERLING L. ROSS, JR. *is Program Assistant,* HENRY G. DEYOUNG *is Program Associate for Program Development, and* JULIUS S. COHEN *is Associate Director, Institute for the Study of Mental Retardation and Related Disabilities, The University of Michigan, Ann Arbor.*

erly. The skilled tester must be aware of the cultural backgrounds of the children and be alert to the anxiety created by the testing situation and to any inability to understand directions because of language problems. Hence, an examiner technically may be able to administer a test and yet obtain results which are not an accurate indication of the child's abilities.

Parents are not given an adequate opportunity to participate in the placement decision. Most school codes require that the parents be notified when the decision to place the child has been reached, and some codes require that a hearing be held before placement. However, parents often are not notified when their children are placed in a special class and are almost never given a formal opportunity to be heard before the placement decision is reached. When parents are involved, it is usually in an effort to obtain their agreement to a decision which the professionals have already made.

Special education programing is inadequate. Once a child is placed in an educable mentally retarded class, there is little chance that he will leave it. Insufficient attention is given to the development of basic educational skills and retesting occurs infrequently, if ever. Contributing further to the lack of upward mobility is the student's poor self image which is reinforced by such placement and contributes to the self fulfilling prophecy of low achievement.

The personal harm created by improper placement is irreparable. Special class placement becomes a basic factor in a self fulfilling prophecy, frequently relegating the victim to an economic, educational, and social position far below that which he has the ability to achieve. The social stigma surrounding the label "mentally retarded" remains with the individual his entire life. Obtaining a job may be difficult if not impossible, and even if adequate employment is found, the psychological damage created by improper placement persists.

The Developing Case Law

The following cases form the nucleus of the growing body of case law in the area of special class placement.

Culture Biased Tests

In *Hobson v. Hansen* (1967) Judge Skelly Wright held that the "tracking" system of educational placement in the Washington D.C. public schools was illegal since it was a violation of the equal protection clause of the United States Constitution. He therefore ordered the abolition of the track system. Under this system students were given the *Sequential Tests of Educational Progress* (STEP) and the *School and College Ability Tests* (SCAT) in the fourth grade and the *Stanford Achievement Test* (SAT) and the *Otis Quick-Scoring Mental Ability Test* in the sixth grade. The students were then placed in an honors, general, or special (educable mentally retarded) curriculum primarily on the basis of test scores. Judge Wright found that in the Washington D.C. schools there were a disproportionate number of black children in special classes and attributed this inequitable distribution to culture biased tests:

The evidence shows that the method by which track assignments are made depends essentially on standardized aptitude tests which, although given on a system-wide basis, are completely inappropriate for use with a large segment of the student body. Because these tests are primarily standardized on and are relevant to a white middle class group of students, they produce inaccurate and misleading test scores when given to lower class and Negro students. As a result, rather than being classified according to ability to learn, these students are in reality being classified according to their socio-economic or racial status, or —more precisely—according to environmental and psychological factors which have nothing to do with innate ability [p. 514].

The chief handicap of the disadvantaged child where verbal tests are concerned is in his limited exposure to people having command of standard English. Communication within the lower class environment . . . typically assumes a language form alien to that tested by aptitude tests [p. 480].

Other circumstances interact with and reinforce the language handicap. Verbalization tends to occur less frequently and often less intensively. Because of crowded living conditions, the noise level in the home may be quite high with the result that the child's auditory perception—his ability to discriminate among word sounds

—can be retarded. There tends to be less exposure to books or other serious reading material—either for lack of interest or for lack of money [p. 481].

Once in a certain track the student is locked in because of infrequent retesting, the student's poor self image, and the teacher's preconceived ideas of the student's academic abilities. Judge Wright noted:

> The real tragedy of misjudgments about the disadvantaged student's abilities is, as described earlier, the likelihood that the student will act out the judgment and confirm it by achieving only at the expected level. Indeed, it may be even worse than that, for there is strong evidence that performance in fact declines . . . . And while the tragedy of misjudgments can occur even under the best of circumstances, there is reason to believe the track system compounds the risk [p. 491].

Therefore, relying on *Brown v. Board of Education* (1954), the court held that the tracking system and its methods irrationally separate students on the basis of race and socioeconomic background and thereby violate their right to an equal educational opportunity. On appeal, the District Circuit Court of Appeals in *Smuck v. Hobson* (1969) affirmed the lower court's decree abolishing the track system.

Discriminatory Interclass Grouping

Since *Hobson,* California has become the battleground over intelligence testing and educational placement. On January 22, 1970, *Spangler v. Board of Education* (1970) was decided in the United States District Court for the Southern District of California. The court found that there was a "racial imbalance" in the student bodies and faculties of the Pasadena school district at all levels. It attributed the racial imbalance to conscious policies and practices on the part of the school district to maintain disproportionate racial distributions. One such practice was discriminatory "interclass grouping" based upon intelligence tests and teacher's recommendations. Without contest by the defendant, it was admitted that the intelligence tests used were inaccurate and unfair:

> The racial effect of the grouping procedures generally in use in the District is to increase segregation. At every secondary school a higher percentage of Black than white students is in slow classes in every subject matter, and a higher percentage of white than Black students is in fast classes . . . . The racial segregation that exists within integrated schools as a result of interclass grouping doubtless has numerous causes, not all of which are treated in the record. . . . One is that grouping assignments are based in part on scores obtained on achievement and "intelligence" tests. As the District's Assistant Superintendent for elementary education acknowledged, such tests are racially discriminatory, based as they are primarily on verbal achievement [p. 159].

Language Barriers to Adequate Performance

In *Diana v. State Board of Education,* filed in the District Court for the Northern District of California in February 1970, nine Mexican-American public school students, ages 8 through 13, claimed that they had been improperly placed in classes for the mentally retarded on the basis of inaccurate tests. Each plaintiff came from a family in which Spanish was the predominant or only spoken language. In the first and second grades the children were given the Stanford-Binet and Wechsler intelligence tests. On the basis of IQ scores so derived, they were placed in educable classes. The plaintiffs argued that (a) the tests relied primarily on verbal aptitude in English thereby ignoring learning abilities in Spanish and (b) the tests were improperly standardized by testing only white, native Americans and therefore related in subject matter solely to the dominant white, middle class culture. This inherent culture bias discriminated against the Mexican-American plaintiffs.

Citing *Brown v. Board of Education* (1954), the Civil Rights Act of 1964, and Article 9 Section 5 of the California Constitution, the plaintiffs contended that the Federal government and state of California guarantee every citizen the right to an equal educational opportunity. The case was settled in February 1970 by a stipulated agreement which set forth the following practices to be observed in the future.

1. All children whose primary home language is other than English must be

tested in both their primary language and English.

2. Such children must be tested only with tests or sections of tests that do not depend on such things as vocabulary, general information, and other similar unfair verbal questions.

3. Mexican-American and Chinese-American children already in classes for the mentally retarded must be retested in their primary language and must be re-evaluated only as to their achievement on nonverbal tests or sections of tests.

4. Each school district is to submit to the state in time for next school year a summary of retesting and reevaluation and a plan listing special supplemental individual training which will be provided to help each child back into the regular school class.

5. State psychologists are to work on norms for a new or revised IQ test to reflect the abilities of Mexican-Americans so that in the future Mexican-American children will be judged only by how they compare to the performance of their peers, not the population as a whole.

6. Any school district which has a significant disparity between the percentage of Mexican-American students in its regular classes and in its classes for the retarded must submit an explanation setting out the reasons for this disparity.

In February 1971, *Covarrubias v. San Diego Unified School District* was filed with the Federal District Court for the Southern District of California on behalf of 12 black and 5 Mexican-American pupils in classes for the educable mentally retarded. The plaintiffs rely on the attack in the *Diana* case on the culture bias of the Stanford-Binet and Wechsler intelligence tests and the resultant denial of the right to an equal education. In seeking money damages under the Civil Rights Act of 1871, they argue that the defendant school district, its officers and agents, conspired to deprive plaintiffs of the equal protection of the laws. In addition, an injunction is sought to prohibit the continuation of special education classes in San Diego until valid testing methods are devised and correctly administered.

Though *Covarrubias* resembles *Diana* in the legal arguments presented, two significant differences are apparent. First, *Covarrubias* introduces money damages as a possible remedy under the Civil Rights Act of 1871, though the elements of conspiracy may be difficult to prove. Second, any revision of current testing methods based on *Diana* must also recognize the cultural influences of the ghetto environment in determining a student's learning ability.

Parental Participation and Prior Hearings

In 1968, 11 Mexican-American public school children, ages 5 through 18 years, filed a complaint *(Arreola v. Board of Education)* in the Superior Court of Orange County, California, seeking an injunction to prohibit the continuation of special classes for the educable mentally retarded until the following reforms are instituted: (a) a hearing is provided before placement as required by the due process clause of the 14th Amendment to the United States Constitution and Article 1, Section 13 of the California Constitution, (b) the IQ tests used to determine placement must recognize cultural differences among students in general and the Mexican-American plaintiffs in particular; and (c) the classes for the mentally retarded provide an educationally meaningful curriculum and periodic retesting.

After *Diana* the plaintiffs' request for more appropriate testing methods appears to be moot. The real thrust of *Arreola* is its demand for parental participation in the placement decision. Before the decision to specially place a child has been made, the parents must be notified and given a formal opportunity to challenge placement. The plaintiffs' argument for a due process hearing was supported by the United States Supreme Court's ruling in *Wisconsin v. Constantineau* (1971). The Court held that a Wisconsin law requiring the posting of the names of alleged problem drinkers in taverns and package stores for the purpose of preventing the sale of liquor to them constituted stigmatization serious enough to require prior notice and hearing before posting. Justice Douglas writing for the Court found the Wisconsin practice to be a violation of the due process clause of the 14 Amendment:

Where a person's good name, reputation, honor or integrity are at stake because of what the government is doing to him, notice and an opportunity to be heard are essential. "Posting" under the Wisconsin Act may be to some merely the mark of illness; to others it is a stigma, an official branding of a person. The label is a degrading one. . . . Only when the whole proceedings leading to the pinning of an unsavory label on a person are aired can oppressive results be prevented [p. 4129].

In educational placement litigation, the plaintiffs are arguing that the label "mentally retarded" is a stigma, "an official branding of a person," the imposition of which requires notice and a prior hearing.

Compensation for Damages

In Boston, *Stewart v. Phillips* presages the most far reaching revision of current testing methods. The complaint was filed in the Massachusetts Federal District Court in October 1970 and delineated three classes of plaintiffs; (1) all poor or black Boston public school students who are not mentally retarded but have been improperly placed in special classes for the mentally retarded; (2) all poor or black students who are mentally retarded and have been denied placement in educational programs created for their special educational needs; and (3) all parents of students placed in classes for the mentally retarded in the Boston public schools who have been denied opportunity to participate in the placement decision. The class (1) and (2) plaintiffs argue that the improper placement of students who are poor or black on the basis of tests which do not accurately measure the learning ability of these students and the denial of educational programs for their specific educational needs abridge their right to the equal protection of the laws as guaranteed by the 14th Amendment. Class (3) plaintiffs argue that the denial of the opportunity to be heard in relation to the placement of their children in classes for the mentally retarded deprives them of their right to due process of the law in violation of the 14th Amendment.

In so arguing, the plaintiffs seek $20,000 each in compensatory and punitive damages and ask that no student be placed in a special class until a "Commission on Individual Educational Needs" is established consisting of members appointed by the Commissioner of Education, the Commissioner of Mental Health, the President of the Massachusetts Psychological Association, and the Mayor of Boston. The purpose of the Commission would be to oversee the administration of a battery of psychological tests rationally related to an accurate determination of a student's learning ability, to devise educational programs to meet individual educational needs, to insure that the tests be administered by qualified psychologists, and to establish consultation procedures by which parents might participate in the placement of their children.

The plaintiffs in *Stewart* have gone one step beyond *Covarrubias* in asking that IQ tests recognize not only the influence of the Black culture in determining learning ability but that they also be sensitive to the influence which poverty has on educational potential. The creation of a Commission on Individual Educational Needs would provide for the continuing revision of special education long after the specific needs which prompted this litigation were satisfied.

Elimination of Racial Segregation

Finally, in response to the United States Supreme Court's mandate to integrate the nation's schools immediately, Sunflower County, Mississippi, proposed that it use intelligence tests to place students in certain schools. Under the plan, beginning in September 1969, children in the first three grades were given the *California Test of Basic Skills*. Those who ranked in the top quarter in test scores were sent to the nearest of three schools. This included all the white and 38 of the black children. Children in the lower three-quarters were sent to the nearest of five schools. This included the remaining 4,100 black children and no white children.

On August 13, 1970, the Court of Appeals for the Fifth Circuit affirmed the District Court's review of the plan which ordered that the assignment of students based on the achievement testing program be rescinded at the close of the 1970 school year. The Court of Appeals held that any use of intelligence tests to maintain a dual instead of a unitary school system is prohibited as inconsistent with recent Supreme Court decisions.

Implications

Special education procedures serve to highlight institutional racism in many school systems. Many minority group children are systematically deprived of their rights to an education. Mercer (1970) examined the process of special placement in the public schools of Riverside, California. She found that three times more Mexican-Americans and two and a half times more Negroes than would be expected from their percentage in the population tested at an IQ of 79 or below on the *Stanford-Binet Intelligence Test.*

Dunn (1968) postulated that minority children constitute well over half of those enrolled in this country's special education classes:

> . . . there are approximately 32,000 teachers of the retarded employed by local school systems—over one-third of all special educators in the nation. In my best judgment, about 60 to 80 percent of the pupils taught by these teachers are children from low status backgrounds—including Afro-Americans, American Indians, Mexicans, and Puerto Rican Americans [p. 6].

Hall (1970) claims there are possibly 15 times as many black children as white in classes for the mentally retarded based on the Jensen report (1969). Franks (1971) found, in an examination of 11 Missouri school districts, that learning disability programs are predominantly composed of white, middle and upper social status children, while educable classes contain disproportionate numbers of black children. The racial breakdown in the educable classes was 34.21 percent black, 65.79 percent white. In the learning disability classes it was 3.22 percent black, 96.78 percent white.

Disproportionate numbers of minority group children alone would not support the argument that educable classes are failing to provide a meaningful educational experience. However, the negligible number of black children who return to general classes bears out the contention that special classes are failing. In a recent study

Chenault (1970) found that once placed in an educable class, it is less likely that the black child will leave the class than the white:

> The exit pattern for EMR students placed in special classes was found to vary as a function of race. This finding is indicative of a school policy which basically retains Black students in special classes once they are diagnosed and placed. Caucasian students, on the other hand, were found to have access to exits such as transferring to parochial schools, moving from the school district, or entering the job market [p. ix, x].

Educators must examine their use of intelligence test scores. Intelligence tests have been under attack for their unfair treatment of racial and cultural minorities for many years. Intelligence test scores and the other criteria currently used for special placement are separating out those children of ethnic and socioeconomic minorities whom the educational system has determined do not possess the necessary skills to achieve success in this white, middle class society. Such children are then relegated to classes containing disproportionate numbers of minority children. The likelihood that their school created handicaps will be remedied and that they will be replaced in the regular class is exceedingly small.

Some test publishers have joined in the criticism. However, when facing attacks on the culture bias of tests, the response is not always in terms of test reform. Instead the argument is presented that tests are merely performing the job assigned to them by general education. Lennon (1964) said:

> Let me offer you an analogy that may help in evaluating this issue of test fairness. If we take a youngster who has suffered malnutrition over a period of years . . . and put him on a scale, we may well discover that he is ten, or fifteen, or twenty pounds underweight. We do not then say the scale is biased because of the deprivation the child has suffered. We take this information as currently and accurately descriptive of an important fact about this child—a fact that can be used to his advantage in planning a program calculated to make up for the deficiencies in his earlier care. . . . I suggest to you that this is the way of looking at a test score. The test is giving us a piece of information about a child's performance here and now, which information if properly used, can be extremely helpful

in planning the educational endeavors of the child [p. 9].

Educators will not be able to continue to hide behind the indefensible and inexcusable use of intelligence test scores as the primary basis for identifying, labeling and placing children in special classes. The psychologists' defense has been that it is not the problem of the instrumentation but rather the way in which the results have been used. The educators' defense is that while test scores might not be the best indicators of mental retardation, they are the most easily attainable and accurate predictor of school achievement. These arguments overlook the fact that the results are not meaningful since minority group children were not represented in the sample group on which the norms were based and that the application of such instruments to them deprives them of their basic rights. Perhaps what should be recognized is that while trying to weigh the child, a ruler rather than a scale is being used.

The interaction of the child and his environment must be examined carefully in every diagnostic workup. Pathology may reside not in the child but in the school. In such situations, behavior judged as maladaptive by one set of norms may be appropriate and necessary. The ease with which the white controlled educational system has applied the instrument, the label, and the stigma of special class placement on minority children is a function of institutionalized racism in the school setting. Educators "know" that black kids are dumb; the tests "prove" that they are dumb; and then the special education programing ensures the kinds of behaviors through which such children can demonstrate that they are dumb. Diagnostic attention must be given to the personnel and to the system before any child or group of children is relegated to other than regular educational experiences.

University training of educators and psychologists must be revised to meet the demands of consumers. During the preparation of this paper, the authors had extended contacts with faculty from many universities and with a great number of students from a variety of disciplines. There was a wide range of awareness about the litigation and its implications. However, primary concern of the majority of faculty was training more psychologists to administer the standardized tests and teachers to work with children in segregated classrooms. Unfortunately, many of the university students reflected the same values. Even programs that were moving beyond this were not fully integrating what must be done to improve special education programing, to break the cycle of built in discrimination and failure in many public school students, and to prepare professionals able to develop and apply alternating approaches to child needs.

There will be accountability for program decisions. It is obvious that educators and psychologists must have a greater concern about the negative effects of the separation of a child from the mainstream of education. Such movement is seen by the courts as a deprivation of rights and it is becoming increasingly evident that due process must be followed in such cases. Parents must be active, informed participants in the decision making process. Special class placement must be demonstrated as an effective tool to assist the child in his education, and placement must not be a one way, school life sentence. Routine review and reevaluations, improved programing, and relevant experiences must be available, and their value to the child must be demonstrated.

Maintaining the status quo will be costly. A final implication of the court cases is that the continuation of the existing practices may cost money. The cases which are asking for compensatory and punitive damages have not as yet been decided. However, if the $20,000 being requested for each plaintiff in the *Stewart v. Phillips* case in Boston is awarded, this will cost the Boston school system millions of dollars. Lest the individual professional feel somewhat apart from this, there has been some discussion of malpractice suits directed at individual practitioners who, because of their own roles in the identification, labeling, and placement process, do in fact engage in improper, unethical, or negligent treatment which results in real damage to the child.

Conclusions

The rapid growth of litigation indicates that parents of minority group children have become increasingly dissatisfied with the criteria used to determine special class placement and with the level of educational programing their children receive after placement. Generally, school systems have been unresponsive to pleas for change, so the parents have turned to the courts. Parents have not been alone in voicing their dissatisfaction. Increasingly, the use of intelligence tests, the viability of special education programing, and the relevance of the total school experience are coming under attack by professionals. Of great concern is the unfair treatment of racial and cultural minorities and the growing realization that educable classes are not remedying deficiencies in children.

The response of the profession must not be merely to protect itself but to serve the needs of children. The response to a court order to prevent inappropriate placements and to remove children from special classes must not result in dumping those children into regular classes without providing for their special needs. Responsible educators must devise special approaches and programs to assist such children within the regular class framework. The actions of the professionals should not focus on behaviors to protect themselves and their systems from court suits; emphasis must be on those actions which modify practices, improve programs, and serve as efficient and effective responses to the needs of individual children.

While litigation indicates the seriousness of the present situation, a basic question is raised: Who will direct educational reform, judges or educators? Judge Wright expressed his reluctance to make educational decisions in *Hobson:*

> It is regrettable, of course, that in deciding this case this court must act in an area so alien to its expertise. It would be far better indeed for these great social and political problems to be resolved in the political arena by other branches of government. But these are social and political problems which seem at times to defy such resolution. In such situations, under our system, the judiciary must bear a hand and accept its responsibility to assist in the solution where constitutional rights hang in the balance [p. 517].

Educators have a final opportunity to lead in the change, rather than have it imposed. Such leadership will require a careful reexamination of the behavior of school staff rather than school children. Each individual must examine his own role and his own contribution to a system which frequently is repressive, discriminatory, culturally and racially biased, and not responsive to the needs of children. Such a critical assessment is essential to the establishment of a personal accountability for what is done to children in schools. People, rather than systems, hurt other people. Each educator must decide whether he will continue dealing with the symptoms or start working on the cause.

References

Arreola v. Board of Education, 160 577 (1968).

Brown v. Board of Education, 347 U.S. 483, 74 S. Ct. 686 (1954).

California Constitution, Article 9, Section 5.

Chenault, J. *Mental retardation as a function of race, sex and social economic status.* Doctoral Dissertation, Michigan State University, 1970.

Civil Rights Act, 42 U.S. Code 2000d, 2000d-1 (1964).

Covarrubias v. San Diego Unified School District, 70-394 Texas Reports (February, 1971).

Diana v. State Board of Education, C-70 37 RFP, District Court for Northern California (February, 1970).

Dunn, L.M. Special education for the mildly retarded—Is much of it justiable? *Exceptional Children,* 1968, **35,** 5-22.

Franks, D.J. Ethnic and social status characteristics of children in EMR and LD classes. *Exceptional Children,* 1971, **37,** 537-538.

Hall, E. The politics of special education. In *Inequality in Education.* Harvard Center for Law and Education, March 16, 1970, Nos. 3 & 4, pp. 17-22.

Hobson v. Hansen, 269 F.Supp. 401 (1967).

Jensen, A.R. How much can we boost IQ and scholastic achievement? *Harvard Educational Review,* 1969, **39,** 1-123.

Lennon, R.T. *Testing and the culturally disadvantaged child.* Boston: Harcourt, Brace and World, 1964.

Mercer, J.R. The ecology of mental retardation. In *The Proceedings of the First Annual Spring Conference of the Institute for the Study of Mental Retardation,* Ann Arbor, Michigan, 1970, pp. 55-74.

Smuck v. Hobson, 408 F.2d 175 (1969).

Spangler v. Board of Education, 311 F.Supp. 501 (1970).

Stewart v. Phillips, 70-1199-F (October, 1970).

Wisconsin v. Constantineau, 39 U.S.L.W. 4128 (January 19, 1971).

Appendix H

Bibliography

Bingham, Walter Van Dyke. *Aptitudes and Aptitude Testing*. New York: Harper, 1937.

A treatment of the method and theory of testing specific traits and a discussion of various tests used for this purpose. Good discussions of testing for aptitude in the vocational education area.

Buros, O. K. (Ed.). *Mental Measurements Yearbooks,* 4th - 7th editions. Highland Park, New Jersey: Gryphon Press, 1953-1972.

Reference books providing factual information about nearly all published standardized tests available when the Yearbook was being prepared. In recent Yearbooks nearly 50 percent of the test entries are accompanied by professional critiques.

Cronbach, Lee J., *Essentials of Psychological Testing*, 3rd edition. New York: Harper and Row, 1970.

A good basic reference in testing.

Freeman, Frank S., *Theory and Practice of Psychological Testing.* New York: Holt, Rinehart and Winston, 1962.

Basically the same subject matter as Nunnally (*q.v.*) but in not as complex or detailed a manner. Very good and useful book for the person who wishes to develop a better understanding of the basics of tests and testing but who is not prepared for advanced discussions.

Goldman, Leo. *Using Tests in Counseling*, 2nd edition. New York: Appleton Century Crofts, 1971.

Discussion of problems encountered in administering tests in a counseling situation. A detailed and somewhat advanced treatment of the topic.

Goodenough, Florence L. *Mental Testing*. New York: Rinehart, 1949.

An historical tracing of the development of methods, principles, and problems of testing.

171

Guilford, J. P. *Psychometric Methods.* New York: McGraw-Hill, 1954.

An advanced book dealing predominantly with the statistical procedures of psychometrics. The book is a useful complement to Nunnally's *Psychometric Theory*.

Hoffmann, Banesh. *The Tyranny of Testing*. New York: Crowell-Collier, 1962.

A critical book on tests and testing. A useful guide to improved construction, administration, and interpretation of tests.

Kolstoe, Ralph H. *Introduction to Statistics for the Behavioral Sciences*. Homewood, Illinois: The Dorsey Press, 1969.

Presents statistics in an understandable manner and includes discussion of the rise in the use of statistics in testing.

Lyman, Howard B. *Test Scores and What They Mean*. Englewood Cliffs, New Jersey: Prentice-Hall, 1963.

A very useful book for an interpretation-oriented course in testing, although it would be useful for those who simply want to know more about test scores. Compares various types of test scores.

Nunnally, Jum C. *Psychometric Theory.* New York: McGraw-Hill, 1967.

An advanced and detailed discussion of the theory and methods of test construction, scaling, and related topics. Excellent reference for anyone involved in these areas. A good complement to Guilford's *Psychometric Methods.*

Otis, Arthur S. *Statistical Method in Educational Measurement.* Yonkers, New York: World Book Company, 1925.

Discusses and describes statistical methods related to testing and test standardization. A knowledge of basic statistics would increase one's ability to comprehend this material.

Palmer, James O. *The Psychological Assessment of Children.* New York: Wiley, 1970.

An excellent book on personality measurement. Includes many case studies. Recommended for the advanced student.

Runyon, Richard P. and Audrey Haber. *Fundamentals of Behavioral Statistics.* Reading, Massachusetts: Addison-Wesley, 1967.

A very readable basic book in statistics.

Thorndike, Robert L. and Elizabeth Hagen. *Measurement and Evaluation in Psychology and Education*, 3rd edition. New York: Wiley, 1969.

A comprehensive basic reference in testing.